Sehnsucht: The C. S. Lewis Journal

Sehnsucht: The C. S. Lewis Journal

Volume 1   Issue 1   2007

General Editor

Grayson Carter, *Fuller Theological Seminary, Phoenix*

Associate Editors

William Gentrup, *AZ Center for Medieval and Renaissance Studies, Tempe*
James P. Helfers, *Grand Canyon University, Phoenix*
Bruce R. Johnson, *Scottsdale Presbyterian Church, Scottsdale*
Del Kehl, *Arizona State University, Tempe*

Editorial Board

Paul Ford	Stanley Mattson
St. John's Seminary,	*The C. S. Lewis Foundation*
Camarillo, California	*Redlands, California*
Robert Johnston	Christopher W. Mitchell
Fuller Theological Seminary	*Marian E. Wade Center*
Pasadena, California	*Wheaton, Illinois*

Walter Hooper
Oxford, England

Inquiries and subscriptions may be sent to:

The Arizona C. S. Lewis Society
c/o Scottsdale Presbyterian Church
3421 N. Hayden Road
Scottsdale, AZ 85251

Rev. Bruce R. Johnson, President
Telephone: (480) 946-4207
Fax: (480) 946-4208

Make subscription checks payable to "Scottsdale Presbyterian Church."
Price: $20 annually; students $10; institutions $30.

Web site: www.azcslewissociety.org
Webmaster: Kirk Sexton, cslewisphx@cox.net
ISSN: 1940-5537

See back of issue for style sheet, submission details, and subscription form.
Published by Wipf and Stock Publishers, 199 West 8th Ave., Eugene OR 97401
ISBN: 978-1-61097-321-2

Contents

List of Contributors

Walter Hooper (M.A., University of North Carolina at Chapel Hill) is a native of North Carolina. He enjoyed a short career as friend and personal secretary to C. S. Lewis and, since his death in 1963, has served as editor of virtually every work of Lewis' that has been published. Hooper has also produced a number of important scholarly works on Lewis, including *C. S. Lewis: A Biography* (with Roger Lancelyn Green, 1974), *C. S. Lewis. A Companion and Guide* (1996), and *The Collected Letters of C. S. Lewis*, 3 vols. (2004–7). He lives in Oxford, England.

James P. Helfers (Ph.D., University of Michigan) is the former Dean of the College of Liberal Arts and Sciences and currently Professor of English and Chair of the Department of Humanities at Grand Canyon University in Phoenix, Arizona. He has authored articles on the medieval mystic and pilgrim Margery Kempe and on the early modern editor of travel and exploration narratives Richard Hakluyt. Most recently, he has edited *Multicultural Europe and Cultural Exchange in the Middle Ages and Renaissance* (2005).

Charles Connell (Ph.D., Rutgers University) is formerly Provost and currently Professor of History at Northern Arizona University in Flagstaff, Arizona. His most recent works include *The World of Medieval Women* (co-editor and contributor, 1985); and, *Literary and Historical Perspectives of the Middle Ages* (co-editor, contributor, 1982). He is currently at work on a book-length manuscript, *Vox Populi, Vox Dei: Public Opinion in the High Middle Ages*. He has also published a number of scholarly articles on medievalism, broadly defined.

Del Kehl (Ph.D., University of Southern California) is emeritus Professor of English at Arizona State University, in Tempe, Arizona, where he taught twentieth-century American literature. His published works include *Poetry and the Visual Arts* (1975); *Control Yourself! Practicing the Art of Self-Discipline* (1982); and,

"Higher Educanto: Doublespeak in Academe," *ETC.: A Review of General Semantics* (1994), 332–7. Recent and current projects include "Thalia Does the Charleston: Humor in the Fiction of F. Scott Fitzgerald"; "*Sehnsucht* in 20th-Century American Fiction"; and, "The Devil Figure in 20th-Century American Fiction."

Victor Reppert (Ph.D., University of Illinois at Urbana-Campaign) teaches philosophy at Glendale Community College in Glendale, Arizona. In addition to a number of previous scholarly articles, he is the author of *C. S. Lewis's Dangerous Idea: A Philosophical Defense of Lewis's Argument from Reason* (2003).

Bruce R. Johnson (D.Min., Fuller Theological Seminary) is Senior Pastor of Scottsdale Presbyterian Church in Scottsdale, Arizona, and President of the Arizona C. S. Lewis Society.

William Gentrup (Ph.D., Arizona State University) is the Assistant Director of the Arizona Center for Medieval and Renaissance Studies at ASU. He has edited *Reinventing the Middle Ages and the Renaissance* (1997) and, with Jean R. Brink, *Renaissance Culture in Context: Theory and Practice* (1993). He has also contributed to the *Complete Literary Guide to the Bible* (1993) and *Encyclopedia of Christian Literature* (2007).

General Editor's Note

GRAYSON CARTER

Welcome to the first volume of *Sehnsucht: The C. S. Lewis Journal*. It would not be inaccurate to describe the journal as having enjoyed a healthy, if not prolonged, genesis. Originally the brainchild of four friends and fellow Lewis "enthusiasts" who met regularly for lunch and good conversation at – appropriately enough – an Irish pub in Tempe, Arizona, its quality and nature has, shall we say, in the succeeding months (and not unlike a good wine) *matured considerably*. While the first expression of that "maturing" has, admittedly, traveled far from our original, modest vision, we also believe that the journal remains something of a work in progress, that there is still more to be accomplished. In short, our expanded (and expanding) vision for *Sehnsucht* includes the recruitment of an editorial board comprising a number of knowledgeable and able Lewis scholars, a book and film review section that provides critical responses to the latest Lewis scholarship in both genres, and (of course) the presentation of scholarly articles encompassing the entire range of biographical, historical, theological, literary, philosophical and cultural scholarship (broadly defined) pertaining to Lewis and his writings.

The timing of this enterprise seems particularly opportune. Interest in Lewis and his writing continues to expand throughout much of the world, both on the popular and scholarly level, especially in the aftermath of the release of film version of *The Lion, The Witch and the Wardrobe* in December 2005. The publication of Walter Hooper's third volume of *The Collected Letters of C. S. Lewis* in January 2007 has provided scholars with a valuable – if not essential – new resource in the formulation of both biographical and thematic studies of Lewis and his writings. Moreover, the time now seems especially right to encourage new approaches to Lewis scholarship – more interdisciplinary and multicultural in nature – that will build upon the extensive corpus of scholarly work that has been published during the past half century or so.

At present, no refereed/peer-reviewed journal pertaining exclusively to the study of C. S. Lewis and his writings is being published anywhere in North America. This is surprising, to say the least, given Lewis' considerable and abiding influence upon literary scholarship, Christian apologetics and imaginative literature. To be sure, there are a number of peer-reviewed journals that publish scholarly material on Lewis, but none of these, however worthy, concentrates exclusively on Lewis and his writings.

Sehnsucht: The C. S. Lewis Journal has found an institutional home at Fuller Theological Seminary SW (the Seminary's campus in Phoenix, Arizona), and it is our hope to be able to draw upon the scholarly resources associated with Fuller in the continued pursuit of this endeavor. Gratitude must also be expressed for the generosity of Ben Sanders and Community Ministries of Tempe, Arizona, as well as for that of the Arizona C. S. Lewis Society, both of which have provided essential financial support of the journal. Publication of the journal has been greatly aided by the efforts of Wipf and Stock publishers of Eugene, Oregon, and thanks must be expressed to Jimmy Stock for all his assistance in the production of the journals' initial volume.

The continuation of *Sehnsucht*, of course, depend on the willingness of individuals and institutions to subscribe to (or to support financially) this scholarly endeavor. Elsewhere in these pages readers can find information on how best to do that. Equally essential will be the interest and willingness of scholars to participate in the work of the journal, through the submission of articles or reviews for consideration, through serving as a member of the Editorial Board, through encouraging their home institutions to take out subscriptions, and through spreading the word among colleagues and friends about the work and mission of the journal. It is the intention of the editors to publish a new volume of the journal once or twice a year, as resources and interest permit. Expressions of interest and support, offers of assistance, and suggestions for improvement of the journal, are especially encouraged.

Reflections of an Editor

WALTER HOOPER

Dear friends of *Sehnsucht: The C. S. Lewis Journal*,
        Congratulations on your new beginning. I understand that you would like me to say something about my part in the editing and promotion of C. S. Lewis' writings. Let us hope what I have to say will be of interest.

I am originally from the United States, and I began corresponding with Lewis in 1954. While I was teaching at the University of Kentucky in 1963, Lewis invited me to come and see him. We met in June and not long afterwards he asked if I would become his secretary. I moved into his house, and began work. Lewis was desperately in need of help because he replied to every letter he received the same day he received it, and this usually took about two hours every morning. His brother, Warnie, helped him when he was around, but he was away for long periods of time. I wish I could have stayed with Lewis for a long, long time, but I had to break off in the autumn of 1963 to return to the United States in order to teach one final term at my university. It was understood I would return to Oxford in January 1964.

Before I left Oxford I had a friendly argument with Lewis—which I think you could say I won! He was worried about what his brother would live on when he died, and this because he was sure his books would stop selling after this death. "No!" I exclaimed. "What'd you mean, 'no'?" he said. "This happens,'" he went on to explain, "to nearly all authors. After they die their books sell for a while, and then trail off to nothing." "But not *yours*!" I said. "Why not?" he asked. "Because they are too good—and people are not that stupid." I think you could say I won that argument—or you would not be founding *Sehnsucht: The C. S. Lewis Journal*!

As you know, Lewis died on 22 November 1963. Although I returned to Oxford in January 1964 it was very sad not meeting Lewis again. But I was not idle. Lewis' brother, Warnie, invited me to undertake the editing of C. S. Lewis'

unpublished writings, and I began work on a volume of Lewis' poems. But before going any further—let me say at once that you would be wrong if you imag-
ined that Lewis' fame was such as it is now. Bishop J. A. T. Robinson had recently published *Honest to God* (1963) throwing doubt on the Christian Faith. This
was a huge "media event," as a result of which publishers were soon wondering
what to publish—orthodox books like Lewis', or subjective, shocking ones like
those of Robinson? The liberals in America were soon claiming a great deal of
attention when Thomas Altizer published *The Gospel of Christian Atheism* (1966),
thus launching the "God is Dead" movement.

It was a difficult time for orthodox Christians. More than anything, it made
me very angry, and I felt that my primary job was to try to keep Lewis' books
in print. But how? Years before he died Lewis had appointed two of his close
friends, Owen Barfield and Cecil Harwood, to be his literary trustees. I should
mention that Lewis left his money to his family, while the job of the trustees of
his literary estate was to deal with his copyrights and keep his books in print.
They do this on a voluntary basis, not for money. Owen Barfield and Cecil Harwood were fairly old men by this time, and because books are copyrighted for
fifty years from the author's death, they needed someone younger to see those
fifty years through. They appointed me a third trustee.

From that point on I saw myself as helping not only C. S. Lewis, but also
two of his closest friends. There is not time to go into all that happened in those
first few years, but I will mention two events that had huge effects. First, when
one of Lewis' original publishers went out of business, it was up to the Trustees
to decide whether Lewis' books should pass to Collins Publishers or someone
else. As Collins had already been publishing paperback editions of some of Lewis' books, they seemed the natural successor. But, like all publishers, they were
hedging their bets, and were not a hundred percent behind Lewis. It is generally
true that every new book by an author helps sell his old books. And so it was
that when Collins asked me to give them a new Lewis book, I made a decision
that could easily have backfired. I told them "You'll get the new book if you re-
print two of the Lewis books now out of print." What cheek! But they agreed!
Secondly, when I edited a new volume of Lewis essays for an American pub-
lisher they—like most publishers—were unsure whether to go with Lewis and
orthodox Christianity or to throw in their lot with the liberals. I was incensed
when they sent us a contract offering to pay C. S. Lewis only ten percent royal-
ties. That is what you offer someone for their first book, and they were treating
Lewis as a has-been. I scratched out "10%" and wrote in "15%". And guess what?
They accepted it!

I would have been out of my depths had it not been for Mr. Barfield and
Mr. Harwood and many other friends of Lewis who took a great interest in their

friend's books. One of those who did most to encourage me was Professor J. R. R. Tolkien. I would have been totally lost without the Inklings. Thanks to them, and many Christians like you, things began to change. The liberal theologians and their followers grew, but so did the orthodox Christians. The world was not as "Christian" as when Lewis was alive, but at least it was clear who was, and who was not, Christian. Many of those who admired Lewis when his works were fashionable dropped away: at the same time many were discovering Lewis for the first time.

Although I saw my primary task that of editing Lewis' writings, I was also working very closely with Owen Barfield on other matters connected with the Lewis Estate. Despite the fact that we worked with literary agents appointed by Lewis, copyright matters were becoming very complicated, and we were finding ourselves out of our depths in some areas. It was a simple matter to write out contracts for books—but in the late 1970s and 1980s publishers were talking about films and merchandising rights. There was even talk about who would own the rights to Lewis' books on the Moon. We had to hire copyright lawyers in New York and London to advise us.

The main challenge facing us was films. We maneuvered our way through the cartoon version of *The Lion, the Witch and the Wardrobe* in 1976, but we needed experts to lead us to what we hoped for—films of *The Chronicles of Narnia*. I cannot sing the praises of Owen Barfield loud enough. All this time he neglected his own writing to help further those of his friend. That good man was about eighty at this time. We had to consider not only the complexities of modern copyright, but the fact that Mr. Barfield was old, and the fact that I needed time to concentrate on editing Lewis' writings. By 1979 it was clear that, to do our best for the beneficiaries of Lewis' Estate, we needed to set up a company to take over the copyrights and keep things going. I think it was in 1979 that Mr. Barfield and I made over our rights as Trustees to the newly-formed company, C. S. Lewis Private Ltd. Mr. Barfield was now free to write the books he had been wanting to have time for. Life became simpler for me too because the company hired me to give all my time to editing Lewis' writings.

Freed from complicated copyright problems, I had far more time to give to what I had always seen as my first responsibility—to get new Lewis works in print and to keep the old ones there too. Seven years ago I began the biggest project I have ever undertaken, editing *The Collected Letters of C. S. Lewis* in three volumes. Volumes I and II have now been published, and I hope God will grant me the wisdom and perseverance to complete Volume III. He is more likely to do this if you add your prayers. And I, in my turn, will pray for the success of *Sehnsucht: The C. S. Lewis Journal.*

A Time for Joy:
The Ancestry and Apologetic Force
of C. S. Lewis' Sehnsucht

JAMES P. HELFERS

C. S. Lewis called his 1955 autobiography *Surprised by Joy: The Shape of My Early Life*. This title refers to the first line of a sonnet by William Wordsworth written sometime after June 1812:

> *Surprised by joy—impatient as the Wind*
> *I turned to share the transport—Oh! With whom*
> *But Thee, deep buried in the silent tomb,*
> *That spot which no vicissitude can find?*
> *Love, faithful love, recalled thee to my mind—*
> *But how could I forget thee? Through what power,*
> *Even for the least division of an hour,*
> *Have I been so beguiled as to be blind*
> *To my most grievous loss!—That thought's return*
> *Was the worst pang that sorrow ever bore,*
> *Save one, one only, when I stood forlorn,*
> *Knowing my heart's best treasure was no more;*
> *That neither present time, nor years unborn*
> *Could to my sight that heavenly face restore.*[1]

---

[1] William Wordsworth, *The Prelude, Selected Poems and Sonnets*, ed. Carlos Baker (New York, 1948), 188.

The allusion implies at least two things: first, the influence of this English Romantic upon Lewis' thought; second, the connection in Lewis' mind between Wordsworth's "Joy" (sometimes capitalized in the critical literature and in Wordsworth's poetry) and Lewis' own understanding of the experience. Some critical attention has been given to Lewis' concept, often termed *sehnsucht* by commentators.[2]

The Oxford English Dictionary definition of *sehnsucht* as "Yearning, wistful longing" illustrates the term's usage with a quotation from, among others, Lewis' *Surprised by Joy* (1955), indicating that for the editors of the OED, Lewis' use constituted an important change in its English definition. Terry Lindvall, in "Joy and *Sehnsucht*," calls it "poignant longing." The term is also applied generally to visionary experiences of longing in the Romantic poets, many of whom depict it as not just poignant, but also ultimately unappeasable, as Lewis does. Wordsworth's Joy, in particular, has been explored by commentators, and also connected to *sehnsucht*. This essay will track the parallels and differences between Lewis' personal sense of the term "Joy" and the analogous concept in the works of Wordsworth.

Both *Surprised by Joy* and Lewis' allegory, *The Pilgrim's Regress*, treat Joy as central to his theology and personal spiritual development. Elsewhere, this has been referred to as Lewis' "non-argument" for the Christian faith.[3] That is, its apologetic force does not derive from logic, but instead from a reflection on the experience itself. As Lewis writes after describing one of his early times of Joy: "The reader who finds these episodes of no interest need read this book no further, for in a sense, the central story of my life is about nothing else."[4] This statement both admits the limitations of the experience, and indirectly expresses Lewis' confidence that at least some readers have, in fact, had the experience themselves, though they may not have fully considered the meaning.

---

[2] Corbin Scott Carnell, in *Bright Shadow of Reality: C. S. Lewis and the Feeling Intellect* (Grand Rapids, 1974), attempts a complex definition of *sehnsucht* (he capitalizes the term) through most of the book, but especially in chapters I, VI, and VII. Owen Barfield talks (in an interview with Clifford Monks of *Towards*) of his personal use of the term in a conversation with Lewis, suggesting that the talk had pointed out the importance of the term to Lewis before his conversion to orthodox Christianity. See *Owen Barfield on C. S. Lewis* (Middletown, CT, 1989), 129.

[3] James P. Helfers, "Surprised by Joy: C. S. Lewis' non-argument for the existence of God," unpublished Power Point presentation delivered at a chapel service at Grand Canyon University, Fall 1998.

[4] C. S. Lewis, *Surprised by Joy* (London, 1959), 20.

As one might expect, Lewis himself defines Joy most clearly. Some commentators have even used the expanded definition that follows as a meaning for *sehnsucht*, but the more Lewisian nomenclature of Joy (with a capital J) seems more appropriate in this context:

> The experience is one of intense longing. It is distinguished from other longings by two things. In the first place, though the sense of want is acute and even painful, yet the mere wanting is felt to be somehow a delight. Other desires are felt as pleasures only if satisfaction is expected in the near future. . . . But this desire, even when there is no hope of possible satisfaction, continues to be prized, and even to be preferred to anything else in the world. . . . [T]here is a peculiar mystery about the object of this desire. Inexperienced people . . . suppose, when they feel it, that they know what they are desiring. . . . [But e]very one of these supposed objects for the Desire is inadequate to it.[5]

Of particular importance are two facets of this definition: the point that the longing can be acute to the point of pain, though it is desired more than pleasure, and the fact that the object of this desire is ultimately inexplicable.

The Pilgrim's Regress as a whole not only defines Joy in the preface, but details Lewis' Augustinian Platonism as well. Plato is the single most-quoted author in the epigraphs that preface the book's chapters; further, the Platonic conception that the material world we inhabit is but an imperfect copy of a perfect reality is crucial to Lewis' sense of Joy's importance. It is this Platonic sense that the object of Joy can only be found in the perfect reality of God's presence that fuels Lewis' reflections on Joy. It is crucial to the apologetic force of this insight that, first, the object of desire be unattainable in this world, and that, second, there be an actual ideal world for that object to inhabit. For Lewis, as for Augustine, Heaven fulfills the promise of Plato's ideal world of the Forms.

John, the protagonist in *The Pilgrim's Regress*, begins his significant spiritual journey when he first glimpses a beautiful and magical island through a window in a wall.[6] Previous to that experience John's religion had been reduced to following rules and fear of punishment. But after glimpsing the island, he begins a pilgrimage to Christianity (with many episodes of bewilderment and wrong turns) that ends with a more comprehensive, though still distant, vision of the island. John initially experiences Joy in terms that one might recognize

---

[5] C. S. Lewis, *The Pilgrim's Regress* (Grand Rapids, 1958), 7–9.
[6] Ibid., 24.

as Romantic. He senses that he had known a similar wood (with primroses) as a child, but, as the passage continues, he debates more and more whether this knowledge arises from his memory, or is an entirely new experience that triggers a memory. Subsequent chapters describe not only his desire for the island (and his realization that even the unfulfilled longing of the experience is part of its attraction), but also his initial acceptance of counterfeits, and rationalizations about the nature of Joy. John's ultimate experience, as recounted at the end of the book, is allegorically described as a completion of the original; at this point, he captures the sight and perfume of the island unalloyed by the terrestrial influences of the primrose-strewn forest. He realizes that the smells and sounds that entranced him at the beginning come from somewhere else than the land on which he stands, and they are:

> . . . mixed with a little sharpness of the sea. But for John . . . the pain and the longing were changed and all unlike what they had been of old: for humility was mixed with their wildness, and the sweetness came not with pride and with the lonely dreams of poets nor with the glamour of a secret, but with the homespun truth of folk-tales and with the sadness of graves and freshness as of earth in the morning.[7]

In the same way, the Wordsworthian sonnet that Lewis appropriates for his autobiography's title does not present a happy resolution to the initial experience of Joy. In it, the poet has a moment of vision. He is "surprised by joy." But it does not bring him the serenity and fusion of past and present he finds elsewhere; instead, his joy is demolished when he turns to share it with the one he loves, and finds that she is not there. In fact, she is "deep buried in the silent tomb." There is no positive resolution in this poem. Wordsworth goes from being "surprised by joy" to feeling almost the worst pang that he ever remembers, "Save one, one only, when I stood forlorn, / Knowing my heart's treasure was no more." Nor is there any way, on earth, to be restored to that relationship. For him, this is a moment of despair.

Given Lewis' concluding quasi-tragic sense of the nature of Joy at the end of *The Pilgrim's Regress*, it may not be surprising that he would have chosen this title for his life's story. *Surprised by Joy* traces the theme of Wordsworth's sonnet biographically, analyzing it logically. Though the descriptions of his early experiences of Joy are important, Lewis sharpens the definition immensely at the end of the book, when he traces the final steps that brought him to faith in

---

[7] Ibid., 171–2.

Christ.[8] During his last throes of perplexity before making a final commitment, Lewis discovers a crucial logical distinction of a personal nature—that between "enjoyment" and "contemplation." Simply put, "enjoyment" is the act and "contemplation" focuses on the object of the act. As Lewis argues: "When you see a table you 'enjoy' the act of seeing and 'contemplate' the table. Later, if you took up Optics and thought about Seeing itself, you would be contemplating the seeing and enjoying the thought."[9]

This logical distinction is crucial to Lewis' understanding of Joy's meaning: "I saw that all my waitings and watchings for Joy, all my vain hopes to find some mental content on which I could, so to speak, lay my finger and say, 'This is it,' had been a futile attempt to contemplate the enjoyed."[10] All the specific images and memories that had characterized Joy for Lewis were only the "mental track" left by the actual phenomenon's passage. The actual object of the desire was much different, and it is the character of the desire's object that makes the experience valuable or not. Joy at its best, then, does not truly focus on the feelings internal to the one experiencing it; it should focus instead on the ultimate object. Thus, Lewis began his final search: he had investigated his mental and emotional life, he had combed his experiences, but nowhere on earth could the object of this desire be found. Instead, Lewis described it as "the naked Other, imageless (though our imagination salutes it with a hundred images), undefined, desired."[11]

Though several moves in this divine chess match remained to be played, Lewis was drawn inexorably to the final conclusion: that God was the "Other" to whom Joy pointed. On earth, the desire remains *sehnsucht*, unappeasable longing. However, elsewhere in his writings, Lewis attempts to picture the fulfillment of the longing and desire. Both attempts rely more on the imagery of place than that of personal relationship. In *The Great Divorce*, for example, Lewis paints the outskirts of heaven as both exquisitely beautiful and too achingly real for his protagonist to experience without pain:

It was the light, the grass, the trees that were different; made of some different substance, so much solider than things in our country that men were ghosts by comparison. Moved by a sudden thought, I bent down and tried to pluck a daisy. . . . The stalk wouldn't break. . . . The little flower was hard, not like wood or even like iron, but like diamond. There was a leaf—

---

[8] *Surprised by Joy*, 174–7.
[9] Ibid., 174.
[10] Ibid., 175.
[11] Ibid., 177.

a young tender beech-leaf, lying in the grass beside it. I tried to pick the leaf up: my heart almost cracked with the effort. . . .[12]

A less disquieting place image is presented in *The Last Battle*, the final volume of Lewis' seven-part *The Chronicles of Narnia*. The heroes and heroines of these volumes find themselves, after apparently losing a hopeless battle, awakened in a far different place:

> It still seemed to be early and the morning freshness was in the air. They kept on stopping to look round and to look behind them, partly because it was so beautiful but partly also because there was something about it which they could not understand.
>
> "Peter," said Lucy, "where is this, do you suppose?"
>
> "I don't know," said the High King. "It reminds me of somewhere but I can't give it a name. Could it be somewhere we once stayed for a holiday when we were very, very small?"
>
> "It would have to have been a jolly good holiday," said Eustace. "I bet there isn't a country like this anywhere in our world. Look at the colors. You couldn't get a blue like the blue on those mountains in our world. . . ."
>
> Lucy said, "They're different. They have more colors on them and they look further away than I remembered and they're more . . . more . . . oh, I don't know. . . ."
>
> "More like the real thing," said the Lord Digory softly.[13]

One feels a certain tension in these passages as Lewis reaches for a description of the ineffable, and falls short. Perhaps he is doing the best he can to paint an Augustinian "Eternal Present," a Platonic world beyond time, through the depiction of place. It is clear, though, that, however much the general idea of perfection in the world of Forms appealed to Lewis, he never found a way verbally to picture (if indeed he wanted to) Plato's (and Augustine's) further contention that time is part of the world of becoming, an imperfection. Plato's eternal world of the forms is a world of static harmony. For Lewis, even heaven is a place of movement and activity, at least for limited beings.

Wordsworth's sonnet that Lewis appropriates, however, only records the Joy experience; it does not explore it. To understand the components of Wordsworth's Joy, readers must turn to a poem that is ultimately a kind of anatomy of

---

[12] C. S. Lewis, *The Great Divorce* (New York, 1946), 28.
[13] C. S. Lewis, *The Last Battle* (New York, 1970), 167–9.

Joy—"Lines Composed a few miles above Tintern Abbey." As a Romantic poet, Wordsworth strove for integrative vision through poetry, as a way imaginatively to reconstruct the world's meaning. For him, poetry was a way to recollect the past, and in a sense to re-create it, in much the same way as John experiences Joy in *The Pilgrim's Regress*. Many of Wordsworth's poems, most notably his "Lines composed a few miles above Tintern Abbey," masterfully illustrate how present sensations can be fused with memory to create meaningful pictures and powerful insights, to consummate the longing of *sehnsucht* (if such a contradiction of the contemporary definition of the term were possible). "Tintern Abbey," among a number of Wordsworth's poems, seems to assert that this kind of fusion can be perfected in one's life.

The first stanza of this poem minutely describes the pastoral scene. Apart from the direct temporal impressions, much of the effect of the time and place is punctuated with the past and memory, beginning from the first lines. Further, the effect of the scene is intensified by the imagination: the "steep and lofty cliffs" impress upon a "wild secluded scene / . . . *Thoughts* of more deep seclusion."[14] In fact, the stanza ends with the poet's imagination of an ideal denizen of the scene—a hermit (with all the religious connotations implied).

Stanza two begins an analysis of how the initial experience had enriched the poet's more mundane life "in lonely rooms, and 'mid the din of towns and cities." He attributes to the memory restorative sensations, feelings of "unremembered pleasure" that influence acts of kindness and love. More than that, he attributes to the memory a sublimity, in which:

> *the breath of this corporeal frame*
> *And even the motion of our human blood*
> *Almost suspended, we are laid asleep*
> *In body, and become a living soul:*
> *While with an eye made quiet by the power*
> *Of harmony, and the deep power of joy,*
> *We see into the life of things.*[15]

The second stanza is important not just for its list recounting the effects of remembering the experience—restorative sensations and moral activity—but also for the first mention of the power of joy, connecting it with sublime vision.

---

[14] Lines 6–7; italics added.
[15] *The Prelude, Selected Poems and Sonnets*, 97, lines 45–51.

Interestingly, the rest of the poem complicates these powerful effects. Even in the second stanza, the poet uses curiously ambiguous constructions—"such, perhaps, as have no slight or trivial influence . . . "—why the tentative and negative phrasing? Or why begin the third stanza: "If this be but a vain belief"? Why look back, in the following stanza, with a barely concealed melancholic nostalgia at youthful experiences, while insisting that the present is more mature? Why pass the torch of youthful enthusiasm, so to speak, to his accompanying sister in stanza five? Thus, the poem gives us a view of the complex experience of Joy, an idealistic catalog of its effects on the poet, and yet casts doubts upon the purity and permanence of the initial description. If we compare this anatomy to Lewis' definition, we find important differences: Lewis makes the movement beyond memory to the absolute "Other" the ultimate goal, while Wordsworth makes memory a vital component of the experience's fulfillment; Lewis does not associate Joy explicitly with the sublime as Wordsworth does; finally, Wordsworth at least ambiguously asserts the regenerative importance and accessibility of the experience, while Lewis sees the experience pointing somewhere beyond its apparent immediate objects.

John Beer asserts that Wordsworth's youthful times of Joy can be traced back to his constant exposure to "the sublime," probably best defined as the Kantian sublime as communicated by Coleridge.[16] Kant's description of the sublime in the *Critique of Judgment* defines it in contrast to beauty: both, he argues, are intrinsic goods, but the sublime, unlike the direct pleasure that beauty gives by furthering life, both attracts and repels The sublime in art, though it uses nature as a vehicle, is an operation of the imagination. The sublime appears to violate purpose, actually "doing violence" to the imagination.[17] For the imagination, the sublime is an abyss, producing fear; reason, however, understands it as pointing to the reality of another realm not directly accessible to our senses. The sublime "raises the energies of the soul above their accustomed heights" and gives us courage to measure ourselves against the apparent almightiness of nature.[18]

One can see the parallels of Kant's description of the sublime with Lewis' descriptions of the nature of Joy. Early in *Surprised by Joy*, he attempts an explanation:

> I will only underline the quality common to the experiences; it is that of an unsatisfied desire which is itself more desirable than any other satisfaction. I call it Joy, which is here a technical term and must be sharply distinguished both from Happiness and from Pleasure.

---

[16] John Beer, *Wordsworth in Time* (London, 1979), 65, 80.
[17] Hazard Adams, ed., *Critical Theory Since Plato* (New York, 1971), 391.
[18] Ibid., 395.

Joy (in my sense) has indeed one characteristic, and one only, in common with them; the fact that anyone who has experienced it will want it again. Apart from that, and considered only in its quality, it might almost equally well be called a particular kind of unhappiness or grief. But then it is a kind we want.[19]

Lewis sharply distinguishes Joy from pleasure and happiness, often seen by philosophers as intrinsic goods—things that people want in and for themselves, and not for some purpose outside the objects. On the other hand, he points to the absolutely desirable nature of Joy as an intrinsic good as well, much like Kant's sublime. Lewis' experiences of Joy point somewhere else than the specific sensory events that trigger it; they also encourage the contemplation of eternity, a contemplation that might well induce both fear and a sense of looking into the abyss. Lewis' idea that Joy "might . . . well be called a particular kind of unhappiness or grief," though of "a kind we want," parallels Kant's difficult idea that the sublime which produces fear is also desirable in some way, a kind of pleasure.

In *The Prelude* Wordsworth's description of his travels in the Alps also illustrates his literary appropriation of the sublime. The elements of repulsion—a gloomy pass, decaying woods, blasts of waterfalls, thwarting winds, sick sights, giddy prospects—point up a powerfully ambivalent emotional reaction. Yet, this experience results in one of Wordsworth's most profound statements of belief in the infinite mind, certainly an experience of Joy in the mold that he describes in the second stanza of "Tintern Abbey." However, this "seeing into the life of things" is not a comfortable, contemplative experience, but in many ways a threatening and fearful one. Wordsworth chooses to express the sublimity of the scene through contradictory clauses and oxymoronic phrases, culminating in an ecstatic doxology:

> *Tumult and peace, the darkness and the light—*
> *Were all like workings of one mind, the features*
> *Of the same face, blossoms upon one tree,*
> *Characters of the great Apocalypse,*
> *The types and symbols of Eternity,*
> *Of first and last, and midst, and without end.*[20]

---

[19] *Surprised by Joy*, 20.
[20] William Wordsworth, *The Prelude*, ed. Carlos Baker (New York, 1954), 306 (Book 6, lines 635–40).

The sublime, then, produces a naturalistic near-theophany; Wordsworth does not see, perhaps, some great Other, but sees analogues ("were like"), or "types and symbols." The experience is transcendent in its way, but should one say that it is a complete moment of vision? Can the moment of Joy be, in fact, completely consummated on earth? The *Prelude* suggests that it cannot.

In "Tintern Abbey," however, Wordsworth suggests that it can, at least momentarily: both in stanza two's analysis, and in stanza three's memory of youthful pleasures in nature, Wordsworth depicts a complete visionary and mystical experience. But he also describes the increasing difficulty of the visionary experience as he ages. In "Ode: Intimations of Immortality from Recollections of Early Childhood," he asserts that "heaven lies about us in our infancy! / Shades of the prison-house begin to close / Upon the growing Boy. . . ."[21]

If one can gauge the progression of Wordsworth's thought about Joy through his biography and literary output, one might talk about the poet's initial confidence both in the experience and in its earthly realization. But upon more mature remembrance and reflection, the poet complicates the experience, adding the more ambiguous aspects of sublimity to it, and begins to doubt that it can be fully achieved in this world. According to Eugene Stelzig, "For the middle-aged poet that thought [that there is no personal immortality] was too monstrous to entertain. . . . And so Wordsworth looked to the forms of eternity and the 'invisible world' conceived in the orthodox light of religion for the ultimate vindication of life on earth. . . . For the later Wordsworth who espoused a type of Christian stoicism, the certainties of stasis and repose are much more attractive than the hazards and flux of open-ended experience."[22]

So, Wordsworth and Lewis arrive, finally, in many ways at the same point. Though it is not clear how or whether Wordsworth ever connected his experiences of youthful Joy with the more conventional religious consolations of his later years, Lewis did. Though Wordsworth implicitly connected the sublime with the visionary experience of Joy in the *Prelude*, it is not apparent that he had thought consistently about this connection. Lewis, on the other hand, was finally driven to analyze this connection specifically during the last stages before commitment in his religious journey. Most of Wordsworth's experiences of Joy came in either interactions with the beautiful and sublime in nature or in interactions with others. Conversely, most of Lewis' Joy experiences came as a result

---

[21] Ibid., 154 (Section 5, lines 9–10).

[22] Eugene Stelzig, *All Shades of Consciousness: Wordsworth's Poetry and the Self in Time* (The Hague, 1975), 192–3.

of aesthetic experience—from contemplating his brother's miniature garden to hearing the music of Wagner's *Ring Cycle* to reading prose and poetry.

In summation, it is clear that Lewis owes a great debt to Wordsworth's idea of Joy, a debt he acknowledges explicitly through the title of his autobiography. Their views of the experience have much in common: for both it is an intense longing, for both it undergirds their sense of the reality of an eternal realm, as well as guiding them toward either virtue (in Wordsworth's case) or a contemplation of and belief in the eternal (in Lewis' case). Both of their experiences connect, either explicitly or implicitly, with the philosophical notion of the sublime. There are significant differences as well; most important is Wordsworth's early sense that Joy is fully achievable on earth. But even this early assertion of the Romantic poet is complicated by his hesitant rhetoric and his later poetic markings of the experience. For both, Joy is fundamental: for Wordsworth, by all the evidence we have, the experience is both crucial and evanescent; he never explicitly connects it to a longing for an orthodox Christian eternity. For Lewis, on the other hand, Joy becomes a crucial precursor of Christian commitment and a strong impetus to continuing faith.

Reading the Middle Ages: The "Post-Modern" Medievalism of C. S. Lewis

CHARLES CONNELL

By study of things outside the poem . . . by steeping yourself in the vanished period, you can reenter the poem with eyes more like those of the natives. . . . In so far as you succeed, you may more and more come to realize that what you enjoyed at the first reading was not really any medieval poem that ever existed but a modern poem made by yourself at hint from the old words.[1]

C. S. Lewis' interest in and study of medievalism have long been neglected. Even among Lewis scholars, the subject of medievalism remains one of the least analyzed aspects of his entire literary and academic repertoire. There is a great need for the exploration of this important topic, not least because Lewis' appropriation of the Middle Ages greatly enriched his work in all of its phases, from his scholarly non-fiction to his Christian apologetic fantasy and novelistic forms. Furthermore, a better understanding of Lewis' brand of medievalism will help to explain the enduring influence that the Middle Ages has exercised on many thoughtful persons ever since the nineteenth century, in both England and America.

The concept of medievalism is complex. There is no definition that readily encapsulates the notion and especially its many exemplifications, from literature to religion to art and architecture. Its nineteenth-century forms were born in the

---

[1] C. S. Lewis, *Studies in Medieval and Renaissance Literature* (Cambridge, 1966), 3.

Romantic movement and Gothic novels of the late eighteenth century and then, during the following century, stamped with indelible force by British writers and institutions such as Sir Walter Scott, Kenelm Henry Digby, William Wordsworth, Alfred Lord Tennyson, Sir Edward Burne-Jones, R. S. S. Baden-Powell and the Boy Scout Code, Benjamin Disraeli, Augustus Pugin, the English Public School Movement, and by Americans such as Henry Adams and Mark Twain.[2]

Much of that medievalism was developed first as an aristocratic reaction to the fears of popular revolution in England, and then as an even broader response to the mechanistic aspects of the Industrial Revolution. The Middle Ages, or at least the idealistic views of it held by these and many other exemplars, was seen as offering something of great value. In particular, Gothic-style secular and ecclesiastic buildings, the "Return to Camelot," the sense of catholic spirituality with its artistic and aesthetic splendor, the personalized society, the sense of order and hierarchy, and the bond between church, monarchs, and aristocracy were all part of the allure of nineteenth-century medievalism. The recreation of a chivalric society tied to land and nature became the model for gentlemen who, it was hoped, would rule England and the Empire during a time that was less chaotic than the now-revolutionary (and industrialized) nineteenth century. The subsequent disillusionment brought on by the failure of chivalry in the spread of Britain's Empire and by the violence and needless slaughter of two world wars produced the context for Lewis' study of the Middle Ages and his own developing medievalism.[3]

Lewis grew up reading Norse mythology of the early Middle Ages; as a teenager, he added Malory, the French version of Tristan and Gawain, the *Song of Roland*, the *Canterbury Tales*, and eventually Scott, whom he continued to read and discuss at Oxford. His undergraduate studies led to a career teaching medieval and Renaissance literature at Oxford and, later, at Cambridge. But Lewis' medievalism was not that of his nineteenth-century predecessors—men who, like Kenelm Digby, studied at Cambridge and were so enamored with the Middle Ages that they created works (such as *The Broad Stone of Honour*) that

---

[2] An excellent introduction to medievalism in nineteenth-century England is provided in Mark Girouard, *The Return to Camelot: Chivalry and the English Gentleman* (New Haven, 1981). Also, see David Roberts, *Paternalism in Early Victorian England* (New Brunswick, N.J., 1979); and, Alice Chandler, *A Dream of Order: The Medieval Ideal in Nineteenth-Century English Literature* (Lincoln, Nebraska, 1970).

[3] See Girouard, 276–93. Compare Lewis' own essay on the need to practice chivalry in modern life. It was published as "Importance of an Ideal," as printed in *Living Age*, 359 (October 1940), 109–11, and retitled "The Necessity of Chivalry," and reprinted in the collection of his essays entitled *Present Concerns*, ed. Walter Hooper (London, 1986; American edition, San Diego, 1987).

urged young Victorian men to adopt a model of Christian chivalry—literally to live by and to guide their actions in reforming society.

Instead, Lewis' medievalism assumed several distinct forms and was exemplified differently in his various works. His study of medieval literature led him to see medievalism as the central, ongoing English literary tradition, and yet his scholarly medievalism was only one aspect that in this case was shared with other medievalists.[4]

Like many other literary scholars, Lewis' medievalism was "reactionary," that is, one that was opposed to the rationalism and scientism of many of his twentieth-century contemporaries. He was similarly suspicious of liberalism, as had been Scott and his early nineteenth-century disciples. In many ways, Lewis was deeply anti-modern. He was, for example, opposed to the methods of philosophy taught by a number of his academic colleagues at Oxford, espousing instead a form of Christian apologetics that they deemed out-of-date, dogmatic, and "medieval."[5] His orthodox views of Christian beliefs on sin, repentance, atonement, resurrection, miracles, the devil, and hell also aligned him more with theologians such as Augustine and Aquinas than with his own contemporaries. Yet, Lewis was not advocating a return to the Middle Ages *per se*, and in this sense one can begin to see how the medievalism he adopted took on a more "post-modern" form.

Medievalism and post-modernism are both elusive terms. Post-modernism has somewhat different meanings depending on the scholarly discipline under consideration. Its origins might be traced to the early twentieth-century work of Ferdinand de Saussure, whose writing focused on the "tyranny of language": the notion that language really conveyed reality or truth as classical education suggested. Saussure's reflections led in another direction: that the "relationship between a word and the object or idea it denotes . . . is . . . arbitrary."[6] Thus, to

---

[4] Cf. J. A. W. Bennett, *The Humane Medievalist* (Cambridge, 1965); Kathryn Kerby-Fulton, " 'Standing on Lewis's Shoulders': C. S. Lewis as a Critic of Medieval Literature," *Studies in Medievalism*, 3 (1991), 257–78; Judith Kollmann, "C. S. Lewis as Medievalist," *CSL: The Bulletin of the New York C. S. Lewis Society*, 10 (July 1979); Charles Moorman, *Arthurian Triptych: Mythic Materials in Charles Williams, C. S. Lewis, and T. S. Eliot* (Berkeley, 1969).

[5] For this background, see Wesley A. Kort, *C. S. Lewis Then and Now* (Oxford, 2001), 14–31; Doris T. Myers, *C. S. Lewis in Context* (Kent, OH, 1994), 1–26; Margaret Patterson Hannay, *C. S. Lewis* (New York, 1981), 130–1, 134–5, 144–5, 156–8, and 180–2; and, Lionel Adey, "Medievalism in the Space Trilogy of C. S. Lewis," *Studies in Medievalism*, 3.3 (Winter 1991), 279–90.

[6] As quoted by John Tosh in *The Pursuit of History: Aims, Methods, and New Directions in the Study of Modern History*, 4th edition (London, 2006), 194. The literature on post-modernism is already quite vast and continues to expand.

Saussure and his followers, language (speech and writing) should be understood as *sui generis*, "a structure governed by its own laws, not as a reflection of reality . . . [but a] structure that determines our perception of the world." Thus, the position of writers is undermined in the sense that writers cannot really communicate "their" meaning to their readers.[7] Following the First World War, many English literary scholars, largely influenced by the behaviorist model of a theory of language advanced by C. K. Ogden and I. A. Richards in their work *The Meaning of Meaning* (1923), were disillusioned with "language-based irrationality."[8] They adopted a "low evaluation" of language similar to that of Saussere, meaning that they were opposed to the idea that "words . . . always imply things corresponding to them." Thus, Ogden and Richards proposed a move away from metaphysicians and churchmen and toward physicists for enlightenment.[9]

It is not clear whether Lewis read *The Meaning of Meaning* when it first appeared in 1923. His declared intention during those student days at Oxford to which he returned in 1919 was to become more of what he called "a realist." As Myers observes, his "New Look" probably "did not involve an explicit abandonment of the high evaluation of language inherent in his classical education,"[10] but he was still engaged in debate over the issue, as his so-called "Great War" with his long-time friend Owen Barfield suggests. This ongoing discussion over the philosophy of language was more influential on Lewis' turn toward the use of metaphor and myth to communicate his ideas and ideals. Owen Barfield, in his *Poetic Diction* (1928), refuted many of the ideas of Ogden and Richards, and argued that metaphor and concept, language and experience, and even poetry and science are a unity because "language is related to nature."[11] Later essays by Lewis indicate his agreement with Barfield regarding the notion that writing about anything other than a physical object requires the use of metaphor to convey meaning.[12]

If modernism means anything like objectivity and the use of language to convey scientific "truth," then Lewis is "post-modern," because he sensed that truth lay in figurative language, in contrast to that attribution of "post-modernism" used by current-day scholars, wherein it implies the adoption of relativism in meaning. Thus, his "post-modernism" is bracketed to indicate his recognition of the role of language and metaphor, and, for Lewis, especially the value

---

[7] Tosh, 194.

[8] See Myers, *Lewis in Context*, 4–6.

[9] Ibid., 6, paraphrasing *The Meaning of Meaning*, 83–4.

[10] Ibid.

[11] Ibid., 8–11.

[12] Ibid., 7.

of myth to communicate meaning. Ogden and Richards took an elitist point of view with regard to audience, namely that metaphor was only for the educated and not the "simple folk." For Lewis, there was a place where the two audiences could meet, namely in the realm of science fiction and fantasy. Thus, his exploration of the medieval cosmos in his three science fiction novels operates in postmodern ways by contributing to the "twentieth-century preoccupation with the nature of language."[13] In *Out of the Silent Planet,* the hero is a philologist; the connection between language and consciousness is explored in *Perelandra*; and *That Hideous Strength* portrays the potential for the use of language as a means of social control.

In providing alternatives to industrial man and asking both common readers and *literati* to focus on the spiritual aspects of life, Lewis' hope for a better life, if not optimism about its potential for accomplishment on earth, is made more clear.[14] In this way also, one can see better the connection between Lewis' postmodernism and his medievalism. Unlike recent post-modernists, Lewis would not entirely reject the possibility of some form of progress, though, ironically, he saw it in the form of using medieval models in his fiction to model a better society.[15] Ultimately, the link is found in his focus on the relationship between man and nature.

The essence of Lewis' medievalism is contained within the medieval worldview, namely, a perspective that things keep getting worse until the end of life on earth, and after that there is a new beginning; in other words, there is a perception of a plan.[16] Lewis' medievalism is concerned with the relationship of man to nature, and its notion of order in space particularly appealed to him. Moreover, the medieval view was at odds with the modern division of the universe into two halves—the natural and supernatural. For men like Merlin, who plays a significant symbolic role in Lewis' work, matter and spirit were one, and every one of man's interactions with nature calls for personal contact with love and reverence and knowledge of nature's spiritual qualities. Merlin also served Lewis as metaphor for another of his medieval ideals, namely, that medieval man was more in touch with the complex secrets and mysteries of nature that only myth could explain. However, in the twentieth century, according to Lewis (speaking through

---

[13] Ibid., 38.

[14] Ibid.

[15] At the same time, Lewis remained highly critical of "moral progress," that is, the idea that humans progress morally through the ages, that they fail to commit the same sins as previous generations.

[16] See the discussion of Lewis' *The Last Battle* in Myers, 174–81.

Ransom), "the soul has gone out of the wood and the water."[17] Nature, for Lewis, was not something to be worshipped *à la* Wordsworth's poetic medievalism. Instead, it was a creature of God from which we derive pleasure as from other of God's creatures, but also like man, a creature in need of redemption. Moreover, this connection of man to nature, the source of the Fall, and of man to the need for redemption was ultimately tied to another aspect of his medievalism, namely, a commitment to the need for chivalry in the modern world.

One of the great themes of nineteenth-century medievalism was the appreciation of chivalry, which Lewis praised in his 1940 essay, "The Necessity of Chivalry."[18] Chivalry, according to Lewis, requires both ferocity and meekness—qualities that the Middle Ages regarded as necessary for lasting happiness in human society. Moreover, chivalry remains important in all societies, even in the "classless democratic" modern world of the twentieth century. The challenge now faced by modern men is that chivalry must be learned independently, since it is no longer a prominent part of the upbringing of the elite as it had been in the homes, private reading, and public schools of the nineteenth century. However, Lewis' concept of chivalry was also informed by his reading of the Arthurian literature, which offered a code of conduct and a court of knights that brought an ideal order to earthly society. His reading of Malory was not naïve, but he somehow remained hopeful. As Moorman remarked, Lewis "envisions a perpetual dichotomy and conflict . . . between Logres and Britain, the Arthurian ideal of unity [under a wise king] and the secular reality."[19] However, apparently Lewis also believed the Arthurian legend had some basis in fact, that is, that there had been a King Arthur who created a strong unified kingdom, one that was connected to nature in a way that offered greater hope for spiritual redemption. So the hope of restoring the same in the modern era could be seen as more in the realm of possibility, as in the case of his use of the Grail myth in *That Hideous Strength* in the form of the Fisher King, half-human, half divine, and ageless.[20] Thus, Lewis used his medievalism to evoke emotion and wonder in order to help his readers conceive a medieval sense of earthly order that might mirror that of the medieval cosmic order, both of which he hoped might inspire a way to restore order in the twentieth century.

---

[17] See Martha Sammons, *A Guide Through C. S. Lewis's Space Trilogy* (Westchester, IL, 1980), 82.

[18] See n. 3, above, for citation of this essay. Cf. the summary of the essay in *The C. S. Lewis Readers' Encyclopedia*, ed. J. D. Schultz and John West, Jr. (Grand Rapids, MI, 1998), 296.

[19] Moorman, 113.

[20] Ibid.

The medieval cosmos fascinated Lewis. The medieval model argued that the universe is a large, perfect sphere, with a round earth sitting motionless at the center, surrounded by seven globes. Each of these globes is transparent and luminous and each is larger than the other and more and more distant from earth, with the closest being the moon and the furthest Saturn. Above Saturn in the order of this medieval universe was a sphere of fixed stars, then came the *Primum Mobile* or First Mover, and, finally, above all else was the infinite Empyrean, or true Heaven. What Lewis admired in this model was not its precise detail but its sense of order. Space for him was not empty; it was full of vitality. Thus, his so-called "Space Trilogy" argued that though earth is at the center of the medieval universe, it is not really significant. In fact, the earth is in a "bent and silent" state caused by the Fall of man in the Garden of Eden, which resulted in a separation of matter and spirit, even of God and man.[21] According to Lewis, man will always be limited in his knowledge because of a gap between experience and perception, and so both reason and imagination (not reason alone as per the modern mantra) are needed to close that gap. The result is a truly religious life, which can only be achieved, Lewis believed, through metaphor, the most perfect form of which is myth. Thus, Lewis employed the post-modern medium of language to communicate, a medium that reunited him to the Middle Ages, albeit in a modified form. Original sin had cut off man from Truth, but much like the medieval call for a leap of faith, man can "attain glimpses of it through myth" because at the heart of myth is "a revelation of God."[22]

As Doris Myers and Wesley Kort remind us, Lewis was concerned with reviving the works of medieval and Renaissance literature by "placing them in the context of their time."[23] His own sense of space as virtually alive and his use of spatial imagery were forms of medievalism that enabled him better to suggest what it was like to live in a world "that is understood religiously."[24] Yet, Lewis' use of space was also post-modern in the sense that he really wanted to direct attention beyond the current modern period to the future and not to the medieval past itself.[25] For Lewis, the best future involved a spiritual awakening and the

---

[21] The "Space Trilogy" is a term applied collectively to the three novels about the nature of the universe, *Out of the Silent Planet, Perelandra,* and *That Hideous Strength.* For a more complete and convenient summary of each of the novels and the relationship of one to another, see the appropriate entries in *The C. S. Lewis Readers' Encyclopedia.*

[22] Sammons, *Guide,* 88.

[23] Myers, ix.

[24] Wesley A. Kort, *C. S. Lewis Then and Now* (Oxford, 2001), 53–4.

[25] Ibid., 54.

end of evils brought about by modern industrialism and totalitarianism.[26] Thus, he used spatial imagery and language to excite the imagination. Importantly, however, his "post-modernism" was not marked by a tendency toward nihilism that much literary post-modernism connotes. His boyhood readings of Malory, Scott, and Mark Twain, as already stated, as well as his professional study of medieval literature, helped him to understand the positive role of culture as a mediator between religious beliefs and everyday life. Thus, he actually chose to write myth and fantasy in order to bring reason and imagination together, to practice what he believed about myth. As Michael Bell, in his study of early twentieth-century developments leading to the post-modern use of language, observes, in "the twentieth century language itself has become the mode of the universe,"[27] or the mode of myth. Lewis used the language of myth to connect two kinds of audience, high and low if you will, to the meaning of an ordered universe and a religious understanding of the world, which offered hope in the face of the chaos of the modern world that he experienced. According to Chad Walsh, "Lewis . . . practiced a highly sophisticated use of language, metaphor and myth in particular. He knew . . . and stated that univocal language—math or formal logic—cannot express religious thoughts. . . . Only the language of poetry, the metaphor, the myth can properly hint at the literally unsayable."[28] While his Space Trilogy is the best example of this use of metaphor, the fulfillment of which is myth, it was not the only way he demonstrated his intuitive understanding of the coming heyday of post-modernism.

Lewis fully understood the nature of the various controversies over language that were then being debated. He engaged them openly in using language in his own struggle against the scientism of the period, while arguing for a medieval (that is, pre-Enlightenment) form of Christianity. Largely devoid of specific theories, his literary medievalism is perhaps best understood as an attempt "to improve the sensibility and to enlarge the capacities of the reader," and not as an attempt to develop and prove a thesis.[29] Thus, he created his own myths in order to improve and enlarge the minds of his readers, and much of his material is "rooted" in medieval perceptions. This medievalism was used to "enhance the sense of wonder or awe" in his readers.[30] His expansion on medieval concepts of

---

[26] Sammons, *Guide*, 72–3.

[27] Michael Bell, ed., *The Context of English Literature, 1900–1930* (New York, 1980), 52.

[28] Chad Walsh, Foreword to William L. White, *The Image of Man in C. S. Lewis* (New York, 1969).

[29] Paul Holmes, *C. S. Lewis: The Shape of His Faith and Thought* (New York, 1976), 13.

[30] Sammons, *Guide*, 19.

the cosmos that are "sadly lost" can be found in both *The Discarded Image* (1964) and in his "Imagination and Thought in the Middle Ages" (1966), wherein he explains the value of the medieval model in restoring to the current world a belief in the "order of space."[31]

In the midst of twentieth-century chaos—war, nuclear terror, and a scientism that mindlessly advocated space exploitation, for example—Lewis argued in favor of a "post-modern" medievalism based on two key frameworks of the Middle Ages, that is, the medieval sense of the cosmos as a model for order in space and the Arthurian legend as a model for order on earth.[32] Since in his fiction he had turned the medieval cosmos inside out, Lewis obviously was not recommending a literal adoption of the medieval model *per se*, but was advocating its examination as a way to see all models in a more imaginative, post-modern fashion.

Language and words were crucial to Lewis, as they are in any post-modern construct. Thus, Lewis tried to get modern men and women creatively to capture the "emotional effect" of the medieval models, to "take a walk by starlight and reject the modern idea that we are looking upon a vast wasteland."[33] As a scholar of medievalism, he argued (as Hannay has claimed, citing Lewis' own argument in *The Discarded Image*) that "To enter the world of the Middle Ages our modern perspective on the universe must be inverted. In evolutionary thought [quoting Lewis] 'Man stands at the top of a stair whose foot is lost in obscurity; in this [medieval], he stands at the bottom of a stair whose top is invisible with light.'"[34] Thus, like the post-modernists, Lewis rejected the arrogance of certainty implied in the modern word of scientism, but did not adopt the nihilism, or the pessimism, implied in the world of post-modernism itself. His adoption of post-modern uses of language and adherence to the creation of tales using myth and metaphor to bring understanding led him to this middle ground of "post-modern" medievalism.

In summary, if one accepts a simple definition of medievalism as "the continuing process of creating the Middle Ages,"[35] Lewis clearly offers us a form of medievalism that is both selective and powerful. He does so in an attempt to offer hope for a future that is built upon positive medieval values regarding order in the universe and the spiritual connection between religion, man, and nature.

---

[31] Ibid., 41–2.

[32] Ibid.

[33] Hannay, 181.

[34] Ibid., 157.

[35] Leslie Workman, *Studies in Medievalism*, 3.1 (1987), 1.

This process of medievalism, of "recreating" the Middle Ages, of helping his readers to walk by starlight through a myth which helps man to understand the "indescribable," is a process that involves "cultural adaptation."[36] Thus, Lewis' "post-modern" medievalism is his response to the modern world of fragmentation and technological chaos. Ultimately, it is guided by his sense of hope, one that uses a "post-modern metaphor for medieval civilization as a place of an ordered Christian society with a focus on the Second Coming."[37]

---

[36] Clare A. Simmons, ed., *Medievalism and the Quest for the "Real" Middle Ages* (London and Portland, 2001), 22.

[37] Scott R. Burson and Jerry L. Walls, *C. S. Lewis and Francis Schaeffer: Lessons for a New Century from the Most Influential Apologists of Our Time* (Downers Grove, IL, 1998), 263.

Grooving a Symbol:
Turkish Delight in Narnia

DEL KEHL

Imagine yourself a writer living in Britain during the late 1940s. You are writing a book for children, but you believe that a book worth reading *only* in childhood is not worth reading even then, and that a children's story which is enjoyed only by children is a bad children's story. The challenge before you is to choose something a witch might offer enticingly to a boy of ten or eleven, most likely some delicious viand, to symbolize temptation, solicitation to evil. What would it be? This was the challenge facing C. S. Lewis as he wrote *The Lion, the Witch, and the Wardrobe*. Only recently, with the release of the Disney Pictures and Walden Media film, has the symbol received much attention, but even then, in most cases, a scant, cursory glance. For such a key symbol, it is important to consider possible alternatives, the nature and history of Turkish Delight, major characteristics that make it especially appropriate as a symbol, and its symbolic use in a major work by one of Lewis' compatriots.

The possibilities for such a symbol seem almost limitless. For example, Lewis could have chosen tantalizing fruit, like that just out of reach for Tantalus in *The Odyssey*. Or it could have been one of the great silver apples, the Apple of Life, that the Witch in Lewis' *The Magician's Nephew,* having stolen one herself and tasted it, uses to tempt Digory, illustrating the truth of Aslan's words: "The fruit is good . . . [but] that is what happens to those who pluck and eat fruits at the wrong time and in the wrong way."[1]

Fruit would seem an appropriate symbol, for according to Cirlot's *Dictionary of Symbols*, the apple "is symbolic of earthly desires, or of indulgence in such

---

[1] C. S. Lewis, *The Magician's Nephew* (New York, 1972), 174.

desires," and fruit in general is "equivalent to the egg," the seed in the center representing the Origin and symbolizing earthly desires.[2] But apples, whether silver or the golden apples that grew in the mythological Garden of the Hesperides, the securing of which constituted the eleventh labor of Hercules, approach cliché as symbol. Of course, there are other more exotic fruits, such as the pomegranate, which some believe was the forbidden fruit of Eden, or the fig, used effectively as symbol by D. H. Lawrence.

Another tempting possibility might be the madeleine, a small rich cake baked in a shell-shaped mold, a key symbol in Proust's *Remembrance of Things Past.* Or perhaps a Dobos torte, a rich pastry with several thin layers of sponge cake and creamy mocha filling and caramel glaze on top, or even a Linzer torte, a rich Austrian pastry with a bottom crust and lattice top of a spiced ground-almond dough and a filling of raspberry jam. Crème anglaise or crème brûlée? Turkish baklava, layers of wafer-thin pastry with nuts and syrup? Maybe a magic gelato or Turkish *dondurma* (ice-cream) that does not melt and drip? Or could not the Witch conjure up some magic ambrosia and nectar, the mythological food and drink of the gods?

Lewis, of course, chose none of these delicacies as his symbol, and probably never even considered them. Instead he chose something called Turkish Delight, mentioned ten times in Chapter IV of *The Lion, the Witch and the Wardrobe,* titled "Turkish Delight." When the evil White Witch Jadis asks Edmund what he would like best to eat, as a bribe for betraying his sisters and brother, he immediately replies, "Turkish Delight, please your Majesty."[3] The fact that the desire for the sweet treat comes from within Edmund himself illustrates not only the Turkish aphorism, "Eat sweet and speak sweetly," but also the Scriptural truth that "one is tempted when he is carried away and enticed by his own lust."[4] A drop from the Queen's copper-colored bottle falls on the snow, "and instantly there appeared a round box, tied with green silk ribbon, which, when opened, turned out to contain several pounds of the best Turkish Delight. Each piece was sweet and light to the very center and Edmund had never tasted anything more delicious."[5] He gobbles down the entire box and wants more, not knowing that "this was enchanted Turkish Delight and that anyone who had once tasted it would want more and more of it, and would even, if they were allowed, go on eating it till they killed themselves."[6] The indulgence puts Edmund in the thrall of the

---

[2] J. E. Cirlot, *A Dictionary of Symbols* (New York, 2005), 14, 115.
[3] C. S. Lewis, *The Lion, the Witch and the Wardrobe* (New York, 1972), 31.
[4] James 1:14.
[5] Lewis, *The Lion, the Witch and the Wardrobe*, 32.
[6] Ibid., 33.

White Witch, who invites him to her castle when he returns to Narnia, where, she assures him, there are "whole rooms full of Turkish Delight."[7] The experience dramatizes Lewis' words in *Miracles*, published in 1947, about the same time he was working on *The Lion, the Witch and the Wardrobe*: "[T]he slaves of the senses, after the first bait, are starved by their masters. . . . Nature by dominating spirit wrecks all spiritual activities. . . ."[8] It is not surprising, then, that when Edmund later visits the Witch's castle and requests more Turkish Delight, he is given "a hunk of dry bread" instead.[9]

Lewis' choice of Turkish Delight as symbol was especially appropriate but not fortuitous, perhaps because he used his "baptized imagination," which he said he acquired some thirty years earlier, in 1916, when he first read George MacDonald's *Phantastes, A Faerie Romance*.[10] Lewis was later to say of MacDonald's novel, "What it actually did to me was to convert, even to baptize . . . my imagination. . . ."[11] Significantly, according to his friend and biographer George Sayer, Lewis told him that in the Narnia tales, "I am aiming at a sort of pre-baptism of the child's imagination."[12]

It is precisely the imagination that uses both conscious and subconscious resources of the mind to create symbol, an object or image that is itself and also stands for some thing or things beyond itself, the representation of a reality on one level by a corresponding reality on another. Symbols not only play an integral part in Lewis' imaginative work, but also in his critical works. In *The Allegory of Love*, for example, he distinguishes between allegory and symbolism: "The allegorist leaves the given . . . to talk of that which is confessedly less real," whereas "the symbolist leaves the given to find that which is more real," a process which

---

[7] Ibid., 34.

[8] C. S. Lewis, *Miracles* (New York, 1965), 132.

[9] Lewis, *The Lion, The Witch and the Wardrobe*, 108.

[10] C. S. Lewis, *Surprised by Joy* (London, 1965), 146. By a "converted," "baptized" imagination Lewis apparently meant a regenerated, sanctified one—an imagination that enabled him to see "the bright shadow coming out of the book into the real world and resting there, transforming all common things and yet itself unchanged. Or, more accurately, I saw the common things drawn into the bright shadow." For further discussion of Lewis and the imagination, especially the relation between imagination and reason, see Walter Hooper, *C. S. Lewis: Companion & Guide* (San Francisco, 1995); Peter J. Schakel, *Reason and Imagination: C. S. Lewis: A Study of "Till We Have Faces"* (Grand Rapids, 1984); "Lewis, Truth, and Imagination," in G. B. Tennyson, ed., *Owen Barfield on C. S. Lewis* (Middletown, CT, 1990); and, "Imagination and Truth" and "Tools of Imagination," in Lionel Adey, *C. S. Lewis' 'Great War' with Owen Barfield* (Cumbria, UK, 2002).

[11] C. S. Lewis, *George MacDonald* (New York, 1986), xxxiii.

[12] George Sayer, *Jack: C. S. Lewis and His Times* (San Francisco, 1988), 192.

he calls "sacramentalism."[13] In a letter of 1943, Lewis writes, "Symbolism exists precisely for the purpose of conveying to the imagination what the intellect is not ready for."[14] Despite Lewis' general dislike of Thomas Carlyle, he may have appreciated the discussion of symbols in *Sartor Resartus*:

> In a Symbol there is concealment and yet revelation . . . , a double significance. . . . There is ever more or less distinctly and directly, some embodiment and revelation of the Infinite; the Infinite is made to blend itself with the Finite, to stand visible, and as it were, attainable there.[15]

Further, in *The Personal Heresy: A Controversy*, Lewis mentions two kinds of symbols, the algebraical and the poetic, which he says, echoing Wordsworth, "comes trailing clouds of glory from the real world, clouds whose shape and colour largely determine and explain its poetic use."[16] Indeed, his Turkish Delight initially comes trailing clouds of pleasure and even potential glory for Edmund, who has been promised he will be prince of Narnia and ultimately king. The clouds, however, soon turn ominous when he in fact receives only "the sweet poison of the false infinite," a key phrase Lewis employs in his space travel story, *Perelandra*.[17]

Lewis' symbol is particularly effective, then, because its place in the real world determines and illuminates its aesthetic use, fulfilling David Lodge's stipulation that "the novelist should make his spade a spade before he makes it a symbol. . . ."[18] Accordingly, Lewis makes his confection a confection before he makes it a symbol of temptation, wisely avoiding the more popular Turkish term—*Lokum*, the word for "morsel."[19]

The origin of Turkish Delight dates back to the time of the Ottoman Empire (*c*.1300–1918). The introduction of sugar in Turkey in the late eighteenth century brought about numerous creative possibilities for Turkish confectioners. According to popular folklore, Turkish Delight was created when a confectioner,

---

[13] C. S. Lewis, *The Allegory of Love* (New York, 1958), 45.

[14] Walter Hooper, ed., *The Collected Letters of C. S. Lewis*, vol. II (San Francisco, 2004), 565.

[15] Thomas Carlyle, *Sartor Resartus* (New York, n.d.), 217. See Walter Hooper, ed., *They Stand Together: The Letters of C. S. Lewis to Arthur Greeves, 1914–1963* (New York, 1979), 433.

[16] C. S. Lewis, *The Personal Heresy: A Controversy* (New York, 1939), 97.

[17] C. S. Lewis, *Perelandra* (New York, 1965), 81.

[18] David Lodge, *The Art of Fiction* (New York, 1992), 138.

[19] When the novel was first published in 1950 and apparently long thereafter, few Americans knew what Turkish Delight is.

ordered by a famous Sultan to create a unique sweet to appease his many concubines, blended a concoction of sugar syrup, various exotic flavorings (especially rose and lemon), nuts (pistachio, hazelnut, almond), and dried fruit. Reportedly, the Sultan was so taken with the elegant new creation that he appointed its originator Chief Confectioner and thereafter served a plate of the delicacy at daily feasts in his court. In the nineteenth century, a British traveler to Istanbul became so enamored with the Turkish delicacy that he purchased several cases of *Lokum* and shipped them to Britain under the name Turkish Delight, where it became especially popular at Christmas.[20] The Grand Bazaar in Istanbul, established in 1453 and reputedly the world's largest market, a labyrinthine "Vanity Fair" consisting of some 4,000 booth-like shops, offers a multiplicity of Turkish Delight at almost every turn, with varying prices for the discerning (or undiscerning) tourist (and even a shop named Aslan).[21]

In the numerous books and guides that appeared prior to—and shortly after—release of the film, *The Lion, the Witch and the Wardrobe* in 2005 (at least eighteen such publications that year alone), the comments regarding Turkish Delight are varied. Bruce Edwards refers to it as "a childish but powerful symbol of the ease with which the faint-hearted can be duped into surrendering their allegiance to an object or person unworthy of them."[22] Gene Veith calls it "a decadent treat," "a candy, something like a gumdrop—a gooey, gelatinous confection rolled in sugar, . . . sickeningly sweet."[23] To Christin Ditchfield, it is a "sweet,

---

[20] For a brief history of Turkish Delight see http://turkish-delight.com/; see also Reay Tannahill, *Food in History* (New York, 1995).

[21] Clearly, Turkish Delight is *not* a "British candy," as David C. Downing refers to it, or a "British confection," as Kurt Bruner and Jim Ware refer to it. See David C. Downing, *Into the Wardrobe: C. S. Lewis and the Narnia Chronicles* (San Francisco, 2005), 166; Kurt Bruner and Jim Ware, *Finding God in the Land of Narnia* (Wheaton, IL, 2005), 28. Rather, it was initially imported from Turkey and only later produced in England and elsewhere, for example by Crabtree and Evelyn of London (as well as that company's branch in Woodstock Hill, Connecticut). "Original Turkish Delight" is still imported by AB Import-Export, Albany, N.Y. (The box reminds us that "*Lokum*, genuine Turkish Delight is one of the most delectable sweets in the world. Discovered in Anatolia, this traditional sweet was introduced to Europe in the 18th century and has become a world renowned confectionary [sic] ever since—rightly called 'Turkish Delight'." The White Witch's ersatz Turkish Delight has not been the only one: Nestle of Canada has produced "Big Turk: Turkish Delight/Loukoum [sic]," a candy bar touted as "The Original/L'Original," while Cadbury of Birmingham, England, has produced a milk chocolate bar called "Fry's Turkish Delight," touted as being "Full of Eastern Promise."

[22] Bruce Edwards, *Not a Tame Lion* (Wheaton, IL, 2005), 124.

[23] Gene Veith, *The Soul of the Lion, the Witch & the Wardrobe* (Colorado Springs, 2005), 59.

gooey candy,"[24] while to David Colbert it is "a soft, sweet gumdrop cube, rolled in powered sugar."[25] To refer to it as a gumdrop or "like a gumdrop" is somewhat misleading because it is much softer, less firm, more delicate than a gumdrop, nor is it "gooey" if that adjective is taken to mean viscous or having a cohesive, fluid consistency. David Barratt refers to it simply as "a particularly cloying, 'moorish' sort of soft candy."[26]

In some cases, there is marked difference of opinion about the tastiness and irresistibility of Turkish Delight. David C. Downing, for one, describes it as "British candy, a jellied confection with powered sugar (not nearly tasty enough to betray one's siblings for),"[27] while Leland Ryken and Marjorie Lamp Mead conclude that "Most Americans find Turkish delight distasteful and regard Edmund's overwhelming attraction to it as just another evidence of his deepening corruption."[28] Walter Hooper offers a somewhat different assessment:

> Being an American myself I know that American readers are at a disadvantage when they first encounter the Narnia stories. They're at a disadvantage because they've never tasted Turkish Delight. When they do taste it, they understand the temptation of Edmund in a new way. For Turkish Delight is irresistible. It's so good that you feel like you'd give your life to go on eating it. . . . [However,] Turkish Delight soon fails you; very soon it makes you sick.[29]

Similarly, Kirk H. Beetz, who claims that:

> Turkish delights are in fact delightful. They are fruit candies, often dipped in powered sugar. That Edmund should want some is understandable, but he is taking candy from a strange woman and, having a tendency toward cruelty already, he is easily captured by the magic in the candy.[30]

Finally, Donald E. Glover has described Lewis' symbolic use of Turkish Delight as a "master stroke," and concludes that:

---

[24] Christin Ditchfield, *A Family Guide to Narnia: Biblical Truths in C. S. Lewis' The Chronicles of Narnia* (Wheaton, IL, 2005), 43.

[25] David Colbert, *The Magical Worlds of Narnia* (New York, 2005), 30.

[26] David Barratt, *Narnia: C. S. Lewis and His World* (Grand Rapids, 2005), 13.

[27] Downing, 166.

[28] Leland Ryken and Marjorie Lamp Mead, *A Reader's Guide Through the Wardrobe* (Dowers Grove, IL, 2005), 46.

[29] Quoted in Bruner and Ware, 28–9.

[30] Kirk H. Betz, *Exploring C. S. Lewis' The Chronicles of Narnia* (Osprey, FL, 2001), 292–3.

Whatever it was in Lewis' childhood, it is in fact now a highly overrated sweet. . . . The name, with its Oriental and romantic overtones, suggests more than the product gives, and Lewis uses this idea simply but with great force in making the Witch appeal first to Edmund's greed and then to his desire for power.[31]

Turkish Delight has at least six characteristics that make it an especially appropriate symbol of solicitation to evil. First, "Turkish" sounds especially exotic, the word itself derived from Latin for "outside" or Greek for "foreign," denoting something different or curious in a striking or fascinating way, strangely enticing. The word "Delight," interestingly, derives from Latin words meaning "to entice or ensnare." The connotations of the two terms, "Turkish" and "Delight," convey the idea that Edmund is receiving not just an innocuous "sweet treat," but the promise of Vanity Fair's worldly pleasure, Oriental and Romantic adventures, ego gratification, power and authority. They suggest the "Far and the Other"—Byzantium, Constantinople, the Ottoman Empire, Sultans and harems, the Orient Express.

Turkish Delight is effective as a symbol also because of its appeal to each of the five senses. Edmund first sees the round box, tied with green silk ribbon, magically appear. Then he touches and tastes (and smells) the delicious confection. In addition, all the while he hears the seductive voice of the Witch; he eats sweetly as she speaks sweetly.

A third characteristic of Turkish Delight is its appeal to the Seven Deadly Sins.[32] Gluttony and greed appear as Edmund tries to "shovel down as much Turkish Delight as he could, and the more he ate the more he wanted to eat. . . ."[33] Likewise covetousness: even after Edmund learns of the dangerous nature of the Witch, "he still wanted to taste that Turkish Delight again more than he wanted anything else."[34] Pride is manifested in the Witch's flattery of Edmund. "While he was Prince," she tells him, "he would wear a gold crown and eat Turkish Delight all day long."[35] Later on, as the children make their way to Mr. and Mrs.

---

[31] Donald E. Glover, *C. S. Lewis: The Art of Enchantment* (Athens, OH, 1981), 138–9.

[32] In his biography of Lewis, William Griffin notes that Lewis came across a list of the seven deadly sins, perhaps in *The Vision of Piers Plowman*, and considered envy, anger, and pride especially applicable to himself. See William Griffin *Clive Staples Lewis: A Dramatic Life* (San Francisco, 1996), 65.

[33] Lewis, *The Lion, the Witch and the Wardrobe*, 32. See also Jonathan Rogers, *The World According to Narnia: Christian Meaning in C. S. Lewis' Beloved Chronicles* (New York, 2005), 7.

[34] Lewis, *The Lion, the Witch and the Wardrobe*, 38.

[35] Ibid., 34.

Beaver's, we learn that Edmund "thought about Turkish Delight and about being a King ('And I wonder how Peter will like that?' he asked himself) and
horrible ideas came into his head."[36] These "horrible ideas"—anger, envy, and
vengeance—influence his decision to abandon his siblings and join forces with
the Witch. Though Edmund was not quite so bad as to want his brother and sisters turned into stone, yet "he did want Turkish Delight and to be a Prince (and
later a King) and to pay Peter out for calling him a beast."[37] Perhaps the deadli-
est of all the Seven Deadly Sins for him is sloth—*acedia*, which is, according to
Thomas Aquinas, indifference, discontent, or even sadness in the face of spiritual good. "Man is made for joy in the love of God, a love which he expresses
in service. If he deliberately turns away from that joy, he is denying the purpose
of his existence."[38] This is precisely what Edmund does in sneaking out of the
Beaver's house and finding his way to the Witch's castle. "He has gone to *her*, to
the White Witch," declares Mr. Beaver. "He has betrayed us all."[39] Edmund has
deliberately turned away from the joy that Aslan brings and has denied the very
purpose of his being in Narnia.[40]

Yet another characteristic of Turkish Delight is its ersatz nature: it is fake,
an imitation, artificial, synthetic, counterfeit, inferior. Devin Brown is right in
concluding:

> Part of the reason that Edmund devours one piece after another of the
> Witch's Turkish Delight, one reason why he 'wants it again,' is because it
> is not real candy but only an imitation. While tasty, it is not satisfying. In
> fact, it is the opposite of satisfying, creating a craving which can never be
> fulfilled no matter how much is eaten.[41]

As Screwtape declares, "An ever increasing craving for an ever diminishing pleasure is the formula. . . . To get the man's soul and give him *nothing* in return—that

---

[36] Ibid., 67.

[37] Ibid., 85.

[38] Evelyn Waugh, quoted in Ian Fleming, ed., *The Seven Deadly Sins* (New York, 1962),
49.

[39] Lewis, *The Lion, the Witch and the Wardrobe*, 80.

[40] For a literary perspective on the Seven Deadly Sins, see Fleming, *The Seven Deadly
Sins*, and Joyce Carol Oates, "The Deadly Sins/Despair; the One Unforgivable Sin," in *New
York Times Review of Books*, July 25, 1993. For a psychological perspective see Solomon Schim-
mel, *The Seven Deadly Sins* (New York, 1997).

[41] Devin Brown, *Inside Narnia: A Guide to Exploring the Lion, the Witch and the Wardrobe*
(Grand Rapids, 2005), 73.

is what really gladdens Our Father's heart."[42] Unlike the other children, Edmund does not enjoy the delicious dinner at the Beaver's house—creamy milk, deep yellow butter, potatoes, good freshwater fish, "a great and gloriously sticky marmalade roll," and hot tea—because "he was thinking all the time about Turkish Delight,—and there's nothing that spoils the taste of good ordinary food half so much as the memory of bad magic food."[43] Is this Lewis' version of Gresham's Law applied to food and, by extension, to morality—the principle that bad money, food, or moral behavior will drive good money, food, or moral behavior out of circulation? Surely Lewis is not generalizing that nefarious behavior will "drive out" honorific behavior, but an important lesson for Edmund—and for us—is the truth of Paul's citation of a proverb from the poet Menander—"Do not be deceived: Evil company corrupts good habits."[44] Another lesson from Edmund's experience with Turkish Delight is one that Lewis reiterates in his canon: that God is the true and only Creator; believers are sub-creators, and the forces of evil are only imitators.

The Witch's enchanted Turkish Delight is further characterized by its addictiveness, a point made in passing by Thomas Williams[45] and Ditchfield,[46] and somewhat more fully by Veith, who notes, "One characteristic of an addiction is that as the craving grows, the actual pleasure grows less, requiring more and more stimulation to achieve the desire effect. . . . Turkish Delight also symbolizes the sense in which sin is enslaving."[47] "Do you not know," Paul writes to the Romans, "that to whom you present yourselves servants to obey, you are that one's servants whom you obey, whether of sin leading to death, or of obedience leading to righteousness?"[48]

A point about Turkish Delight perhaps not widely known is that, during the late nineteenth and early twentieth centuries, government officials in India and Egypt became alarmed at the large numbers of inhabitants who used hashish directly or in confections exported to Europe. "Among the variety of confectionery treats containing hashish that were sent abroad were 'Turkish Delight,' square pieces of hashish containing sugar and gelatin which were a particular

---

[42] C. S. Lewis, *The Screwtape Letters* (San Francisco, 2001), 44–5.

[43] Lewis, *The Lion, The Witch and the Wardrobe*, 70–1, 84.

[44] I Corinthians 15:33.

[45] Thomas Williams, *The Heart of the Chronicles of Narnia* (Nashville, 2005), 48.

[46] Ditchfield, 42.

[47] Veith, 61.

[48] Romans 6:16.

favorite of the students at Cambridge University in England. . . ."[49] Apparently isolated cases gave the impression that hashish was rampant in parts of England:

> One such case took place in 1886 in the dormitories of staid old Cambridge University. According to a newspaper report, some students had obtained 'Turkish Delight' and, not being experienced users of the hashish-laden confection, had taken an overdose and became ill as a result. Oxford also had its share of hashish users.[50]

Could it be that Lewis, who first went up to Oxford in 1916, returned briefly in 1917, and returned again in 1919 after his stint in the war, then was a fellow and don at Oxford from 1925 until 1954, after which he was (until 1963) professor at Cambridge, knew of the reported hashish connection and chose Turkish Delight as symbol, among other reasons, because of the addiction tie-in?

A sixth characteristic of Turkish Delight that makes it an especially appropriate symbol for Lewis' purposes is its applicability to major themes in his canon. Assuredly, one of the major motifs, if not the central one, in Lewis' work is *Sehnsucht*, a compound German word from *sehnen*, "to long for" and *sucht*, "addiction"—addiction of (or to) longing. Rooted in German Romanticism (for example, Goethe, Schiller, Novalis) and sometimes described by Lewis as "Joy," *Sehnsucht* is a longing characterized by intensity, inexplicability, and bittersweetness. Edmund's inordinate longing for Turkish Delight, his insatiable appetite, his uncontrollable obsession demonstrate the depraved or sinful human tendency to attempt to satisfy a legitimate longing for transcendence, for the numinous, by gorging himself with the poisonous, addictive *Lokum*.

A related motif recurring in Lewis' work is that of desire and pleasure wrongly used, perverted. In his discussion of Milton and Augustine in *A Preface to Paradise Lost*, Lewis attributes to those two writers the doctrine that "What we call bad things are good things perverted. This perversion arises when a conscious creature becomes more interested in itself than in God and wishes to exist 'on its own'."[51] Further, Lewis notes that from this doctrine it follows that "good can exist without evil . . . but not evil without good."[52] Edmund's addiction to Turkish Delight demonstrates that evil has no existence of itself but is a

---

[49] See *The Lewis Legacy: Newsletter of the C. S. Lewis Foundation*, Winter 1996, gleaned from Ernest L. Abel, *Marihuana: The First Twelve Thousand Years* (New York, 1980), which in turn cited Thomas Clifford Albutt, ed., *A System of Medicine* (1900).

[50] Ibid.

[51] C. S. Lewis, *A Preface to Paradise Lost* (New York, 1966), 66.

[52] Ibid., 67.

parasite on good, and that turning from what he knows to be right is the absence of good. As Wesley A. Kort has pointed out, pleasure itself is a major, recurring topic in Lewis' work.[53] Legitimate pleasure rightly used counters self-preoccupation, directing us to the value of something outside ourselves, as Kort notes. Yet, ironically, the attempt to experience wrong pleasure, or even legitimate pleasure wrongly used, feeds on self-preoccupation, as demonstrated by Edmund's increasing self-centeredness and cruelty.

Lewis' use of Turkish Delight as symbol was not the first time the confection appeared as symbol in a work of modern literature; Lewis' Irish compatriot James Joyce used it in the story "A Mother," from *Dubliners*, published in 1916.[54] If Narnia suffers from the curse of "always winter" but "never Christmas," Joyce's Dublin suffers from the curse of political, cultural, and interpersonal paralysis. Joyce paints a disturbing portrait of Miss Devlin, who had been educated "in a high-class convent, where she learned French and music." Because of her "unbending" manner, she made few friends at school. When she came to marriage age:

> . . . she sat amid the chilly circle of her accomplishments, waiting for some suitor to brave it and offer her a brilliant life. But the young men whom she met were ordinary and she gave them no encouragement, trying to console her romantic desires by eating a great deal of Turkish Delight in secret.[55]

Forced to suppress her romantic fancies, she marries an older man "out of spite," thinking that "such a man would wear better than a romantic person, but she

---

[53] Wesley A. Kort, *C. S. Lewis Then and Now* (New York, 2001), 122.

[54] This parallel is not intended to suggest influence. It is not definite that Lewis had read *Dubliners*, although Roger Lancelyn Green and Walter Hooper note that he had read *Ulysses* and dismissed Joyce and Lawrence "to a friend of similar tastes as 'good, I'm sure—but not for us . . .'." See Roger Lancelyn Green and Walter Hooper, *C. S. Lewis: A Biography* (New York, 1974), 291, 152. Similarly, A. N. Wilson alleges that Lewis "appears to have chosen to turn a blind eye to these authors [Pound, Eliot, Joyce], justifying his ignorance of the 'moderns' in ideological, rather than aesthetic, terms." See A. N. Wilson, *C. S. Lewis: A Biography* (New York, 1990), 79. Joe R. Christopher concludes that "a passing reference [to Joyce] in an essay in 1939, 'High and Low Brows,' does not prove Lewis has read Joyce, but certainly he knows of him. . . ." Christopher then cites a critic who wrote, "rather snidely, 'With a sure scent for the real peril, Mr. Lewis saw a supreme danger to Milton's literary reputation in the public response to Joyce'," and concludes: "He is right insofar as the analysis belongs to the moralistic side of Lewis." See Joe R. Christopher, "Modern Literature" in Thomas L. Martin, ed., *Reading the Classics with C. S. Lewis* (Grand Rapids, 2000), 245–64.

[55] James Joyce, "A Mother," in *Dubliners* (New York, 1962), 136–7.

never put her own romantic ideas away." In time, she came to respect her husband "in the same way as she respected the General Post Office, as something large, secure and fixed; and though she knew the small number of his talents she appreciated his abstract value as a male."[56] Seizing the opportunity to manage her daughter's talent as an accompanist, the mother sacrifices her daughter's career with her unreasonable, intemperate concern for money.

Miss Devlin shares a number of Edmund's foibles, not the least of which is her consumption of "a great deal of Turkish Delight," symbol of ersatz romantic fulfillment. Each succumbs to a grandiose illusion—Miss Devlin that she will be swept off her feet by a romantic, high class suitor, Edmund that he will be prince of Narnia and eventually king. If Edmund is puerile, gullible, naïve, conniving, rebellious, unfaithful, proud, and cruel, Miss Devlin is spiteful, condescending, domineering, opportunistic, manipulative, conniving, pretentious, and contemptuous. If Edmund demonstrates all of the seven deadly sins (except perhaps lust), the deadly sins encountered in Joyce's story are pride, wrath, and covetousness.[57] Her anger is mentioned at least six times—"She stood still for an instant like an angry stone image . . . "—and exhibits avarice, lust, envy, gluttony and sloth (*acedia*), all of the deadly sins.[58] If Turkish Delight symbolizes solicitation to evil for Edmund, it symbolizes an attempt to escape unpleasant reality for Miss Devlin, a way to cope with frustrated romantic fancies.

Perhaps the most significant distinction between the two stories is that Edmund, through the influence of Aslan, comes to see the illusion of Turkish Delight and repents, whereas Mrs. Kearney (the married name of Miss Devlin) shows no remorse, portraying a mother who failed miserably, both as mother to her daughter Katherine and as mother of cultural Ireland. Edmund is seen walking and talking with Aslan, a conversation which, we are told, he never forgot,[59] and one which leads him to apologize to his sisters, brother, and to the Narnians, whereas Mrs. Kearney goes off in a fit of rage and a threat, announcing "I'm not done with you yet."[60] Joyce's story ends with poignant irony: "O, she's a nice lady!,"[61] whereas Edmund is dubbed "Edmund the Just," "a graver and quieter

---

[56] Ibid., 141.
[57] William York Tindall, *A Readers Guide to James Joyce* (New York, 1970), 38.
[58] Joyce, 149.
[59] Lewis, *The Lion, the Witch and the Wardrobe*, 135.
[60] Joyce, 149.
[61] Ibid.

man than Peter, and great in council and judgement."[62] Perhaps even greater irony lies in the fact that it is Edmund who has a clear epiphany about good and evil, rather than Joyce's character. But surely the greatest epiphany is that experienced by the reader of both stories, thanks to the symbology of Turkish Delight.

---

[62] Lewis, *The Lion, the Witch and the Wardrobe*, 181.

Defending the Dangerous Idea: An Update on C. S. Lewis' Argument from Reason

VICTOR REPPERT

While C. S. Lewis' argument against naturalism (all phenomena have only natural and never nonphysical or supernatural causes), found in the third chapter of *Miracles: A Preliminary Study*,[1] has interested this author since he started reading Lewis at the age of 18, his participation in the serious discussion of the argument began as a graduate student at the University of Illinois at Champaign-Urbana. Although this argument is widely thought to have been undermined by Elizabeth Anscombe's criticisms (and indeed it is sometimes claimed that Lewis was considerably weakened as an apologist by this exchange), this author thought that an adequately reformulated version of the argument could surmount Anscombe's objections. This claim was defended for the first time in print in "'The Lewis-Anscombe Controversy': A Discussion of the Issues," which appeared in *Christian Scholar's Review* in 1989.[2] This research into the Lewis-Anscombe exchange argues that:

1. Anscombe provided some legitimate objections to the formulation of the argument against naturalism as found in the first edition of Lewis' *Miracles*.

2. Lewis seems to have felt discouraged in the immediate aftermath of the exchange, as shown by comments he made to literary friends.

---

[1] C. S. Lewis, *Miracles: A Preliminary Study* (San Francisco: Harper and Row, 1960), 12–24.
[2] See Victor Reppert, "'The Lewis-Anscombe Controversy': A Discussion of the Issues," *Christian Scholar's Review*, 19 (September 1989), 32–48.

3. Lewis did not think that Anscombe's considerations put the naturalist in the clear; in fact, he employed her distinctions in the response that appears in the same issue of the *Socratic Digest* in which Anscombe's paper appeared.

4. Anscombe considered the revised argument much more serious than the first edition of Lewis' *Miracles*, although she did not endorse it.

5. Although Lewis published no more books of Christian apologetics after the Anscombe exchange, he did write many articles devoted to apologetics, including revising and expanding the controversial chapter of *Miracles* for the Fontana edition.

6. Attempts to identify the Green Witch of the Underland of Narnia (The Silver Chair), who attempts to persuade the children that the Overworld does not exist, with Anscombe are complete and utter nonsense.[3]

Although C. S. Lewis criticized naturalism by arguing that it is inconsistent with the possibility of rational inference in *Miracles*, he did not give the kind of full description of rational inference that he did in an essay entitled "Why I am Not a Pacifist," which is found in the volume *The Weight of Glory and Other Essays*:

> Now any concrete train of reasoning involves three elements: Firstly, there is the reception of facts to reason about. These facts are received either from our own senses, or from the report of other minds; that is, either experience or authority supplies us with our material. But each man's experience is so limited that the second source is the more usual; of every hundred facts upon which to reason, ninety-nine depend on authority. Secondly, there is the direct, simple act of the mind perceiving self-evident truth, as when we see that if A and B both equal C, then they equal each other. This act I call intuition. Thirdly, there is an art or skill of arranging the facts so as to yield a series of such intuitions, which linked together, produce a proof of the truth of the propositions we are considering. Thus, in a geometrical

---

[3] See Victor Reppert, "The Green Witch and the Great Debate: Freeing Narnia from the Spell of the Lewis-Anscombe Legend," in *The Chronicles of Narnia and Philosophy: The Lion, the Witch and the Worldview*, ed. Gregory Bassham and Jerry L. Walls (Peru, Ill.: Open Court, 2005), 260–72. A full discussion of the Lewis-Anscombe debate is found in my *C. S. Lewis's Dangerous Idea: In Defense of the Argument from Reason* (Downer's Gorve: Ill.: InterVarsity Press, 2003), 45–71.

proof each step is seen by intuition, and to fail to see it is to be not a bad geometrician but an idiot. The skill comes in arranging the material into a series of intuitable "steps". Failure to do this does not mean idiocy, but only lack of ingenuity or invention. Failure to follow it need not mean idiocy, but either inattention or a defect of memory which forbids us to hold all the intuitions together.[4]

So for Lewis there are three steps in a rational inference: 1) reception of fact to think about, 2) intuition of a necessary logical truth or principle, and 3) arrangement of those fact to prove the conclusion. In what follows I will be discussing three of the six arguments that I have managed to spin out of Lewis' argument against naturalism. The reception of facts to think about requires that our thoughts be about something, and that is what corresponds to my argument from intentionality. Arranging statements to reach a conclusion requires mental causation, and so corresponds to my argument from mental causation. To perceive intuitively the necessity of a logical truth requires, among other things, the unity of consciousness, and so that argument corresponds to the part of Lewis' description that makes reference to intuition. Each of these presents a considerable difficulty with which the philosophical naturalist has not adequately come to terms, and each represents an expansion of Lewis' original argument, which is simply used as a jumping-off point in this article. Further, Richard Carrier's criticisms of these arguments are not adequate and do not get the naturalist off the hook.[5]

The argument from intentionality claims that our thoughts are about other things. Philosophers today refer to this "aboutness" as intentionality. My book developed an "argument from intentionality," according to which we have good reason to reject a naturalistic world-view because naturalism cannot account for the fact that our thoughts are about other things. In particular, by looking at the necessary conditions for rational inference, special attention is paid to how our thoughts can be about other things at those moments when we have what philosophers refer to as propositional attitudes. A propositional attitude may be any of the following: a belief that proposition p is true, doubting that proposition p is true, hoping that p is true, wanting p to be false, or something like that.

Physical states have physical characteristics, but how can it be a characteristic of, say, some physical state of a person's brain, that it is concerned or thinks about dogs Boots and Frisky, or about late Uncle Stanley, or even about the

---

[4] C. S. Lewis, *The Weight of Glory and Other Essays* (New York: Macmillan, 1962), 34.

[5] Richard C. Carrier, "Critical Review of Victor Reppert's Defense of the Argument from Reason," 2004, http://www.infidels.org/library/modern/richard_carrier/reppert.html.

number 2? If thoughts are purely physical, can we not describe a person's brain and its activities without having any clue as to what his or her thoughts are about? It is important to draw a further distinction, in this case between original intentionality, which is intrinsic to the person possessing the intentional state, and derived or borrowed intentionality, which is found in maps, words, or computers. Maps, for example, have the meaning that they have, not in themselves, but in relation to other things that possess original intentionality, such as human persons. There can be no question that physical systems, such as computers, possess derived intentionality. But if they possess derived intentionality in virtue of other things that may or may not be physical systems, this does not really solve the materialist's problem.

The problem facing a physicalist account of intentionality is presented very forcefully by John Searle:

> Any attempt to reduce intentionality to something nonmental will always fail because it leaves out intentionality. Suppose for example that you had a perfect causal account of the belief that water is wet. This account is given by stating the set of causal relations in which a system stands to water and to wetness and these relations are entirely specified without any mental component. The problem is obvious: a system could have all those relations and still not *believe* [emphasis added] that water is wet. . . . You cannot reduce intentional content . . . to something else, because if you did they would be something else, and it is not something else.[6]

Put simply the point is this. The basic stuff of the physical universe cannot, according to naturalism, possess intentionality. If a physical thing is about some other thing, then that "aboutness" has to be arranged by the basic stuff of the universe. However, any "adding up" of physical states is not sufficient to create an intentional state. There is nothing about physical states, however complexly arranged, that would be sufficient to produce a thought about Uncle Stanley and not Aunt Frances. Searle also writes:

> So far no attempt at naturalizing content [of the mind] has produced an explanation (analysis, reduction) of intentional content that is even remotely plausible. A symptom that something is radically wrong with the project is that intentional notions are inherently normative. They set standards of truth, rationality, consistency, etc., and there is no way that these standards

---

[6] John Searle, *The Re-Discovery of the Mind* (Cambridge, 1992), 51.

can be intrinsic to a system consisting entirely of brute, blind, noninten-tional causal relations. There is no mean [middle] component to billiard ball causation. Darwinian biological attempts at naturalizing content [i.e., consciousness] try to avoid this problem by appealing to what they suppose is the inherently teleological [i.e., purposeful], normative character of bio-logical evolution. But this is a very deep mistake. There is nothing norma-tive or teleological about Darwinian evolution. Indeed, Darwin's major contribution was precisely to remove purpose and teleology from evolu-tion, and substitute for it purely natural forms of selection.[7]

Why does intentionality fail to fit into a naturalist world-view? First and fore-most, *intentionality requires consciousness*. There are physical things (such as com-puters) that behave in ways such that, in order to predict their behavior, it be-hooves us to act as if they were intentional systems. For example, if a person is playing chess against a computer, and he is trying to figure out what to expect it to play, then he is probably going to look for the moves he thinks are good and expects the computer to play. He acts as if the computer were conscious, even though he knows that it has no more consciousness than a tin can. Similarly, we can look at the way bees dance and describe it in intentional terms; the mo-tions in which the bees engage enable other bees to go where the pollen is, but it does not seem plausible to attribute a conscious awareness of the information being sent in the course of the dance. We can look at the bees as if they were consciously giving one another information, but the intentionality is an as-if in-tentionality, not the kind of intentionality we find in conscious agents. As Colin McGinn writes:

> I doubt that the self-same kind of content possessed by a conscious percep-tual experience, say, could be possessed independently of consciousness; such content seems essentially conscious, shot through with subjectivity. This is because of the Janus-faced character of conscious content: it involves presence to the subject, and hence a subjective point of view. Remove the inward-looking face and you remove something integral—what the world seems like to the subject.[8]

If we ask what the meaning of a word is, the meaning of that word must be the meaning for some conscious agent; how that conscious agent understands the

---

[7] Ibid., 50–51.
[8] Colin McGinn, *The Problem of Consciousness* (Oxford, 1991), 34.

word. There may be other concepts of meaning, but those concepts are parasitical on the concept of meaning that I use in referring to states of mind found in a conscious agent. Put another way, my paradigm for understanding these concepts is my life as a conscious agent. If we make these words refer to something that occurs without consciousness, it seems that we are using them by way of analogy with their use in connection with our conscious life. Meaning, quite simply, requires a point of view of a person for which, say, a word means something.

Richard Carrier's responses to the argument from intentionality are symptomatic of the problems that a physicalist faces when he attempts to reduce intentionality to states of the world that are about nothing. His job is to show how physical states can be sufficient for intentional states. Yet whenever he presents an analysis of mental states in physical terms all he does is analyze mental states in terms that are just as mental as the ones he is analyzing. So, for example, he analyzes intentional states in terms of it being a virtual model. But we only know what a virtual model is if we know what it is for one state to be about another state.

Consider his main definition of "aboutness":

> Cognitive science has established that the brain is a computer that constructs and runs virtual models. All conscious states of mind consist of or connect with one or more virtual models. The relation these virtual models have to the world is that of corresponding or not corresponding to actual systems in the world. Intentionality is an assignment (verbal or attentional) of a relation between the virtual models and the (hypothesized) real systems. Assignment of relation is a decision (conscious or not), and such decisions, as well as virtual models and actual systems, and patterns of correspondence between them, all can and do exist in naturalism, yet these four things are all that are needed for Proposition 1 [that there are physical states that are about other things] to be true.[9]

But what we have is a lot of talk, in scientific jargon, that analyzes "aboutness" in terms of states that have the same characteristic of aboutness. It is like trying to give a physicalistic explanation of the effectiveness of a sleeping pill in terms of its "dormative virtue." If we wonder "why is there any intentionality at all," it won't do to explain it in other intentional terms, even if the intentionality is attributed to the brain. Or consider the following: "Returning to my earlier definition of aboutness, as long as we can know that 'element A of model B is

---

[9] Carrier, op. cit.

hypothesized to correspond to real item C in the universe' we have intentionality, we have a thought that is about a thing."[10] Or: "Because the verbal link that alone completely establishes aboutness – the fact of being 'hypothesized' – is something that many purely mechanical computers do."[11] Or again:

> Language is a tool – it is a convention invented by humans. Reality does not tell us what a word means. We decide what aspects of reality a word will refer to. Emphasis here: we decide. We create the meaning for words however we want. The universe has nothing to do with it – except in the trivial sense that we (as computational machines) are a part of the universe.[12]

Now simply consider the words "hypothesize" and "decide" that he uses in these passages. In order to decide something as a conscious agent, I am aware of choice 1 and choice 2; I deliberate about it; and, then I consciously choose 1 as opposed to 2, or vice versa. All of this requires that a conscious agent knows what his or her thoughts are about. That is why Carrier's explaining intentionality in terms like these has been rather puzzling; such terms mean something only if we know what our thoughts are about. The same thing goes for hypothesizing. A hypothesis (such as, all the houses in this subdivision were built by the same builder) can be formed only if I know what the terms of the hypothesis mean; in other words, only if I already possess intentionality. That is what "hypothesize" and "decide" mean to most people. So, any attempt to naturalize intentionality will end up bringing intentionality in through the back door, just as Carrier's account does. When a new or unfamiliar attempt to account for intentionality naturalistically is encountered, it must be examined very carefully; the reader should be able to find out where the contradictions are buried.

Other naturalists have been more modest in the way in which they reconcile intentionality and naturalism. They admit that intentional states may not be reducible to physical states, as Carrier appears to be arguing, but they think that these states are supervenient or extraneous upon physical states. While the mental states are not identical to the physical states, given the reality of the physical, somehow it is necessary that the mental states exist and are produced by the physical, even though we cannot see why the mental states are necessary. However, by admitting there is a mystery as to how intentional states can exist in a

---

[10] Ibid.
[11] Ibid.
[12] Ibid.

physicalistic universe, naturalists run the risk of making propositional states epi-phenomenal, that is, causally irrelevant. While mental states might exist on this view, all causal interaction has to be physical causation. Therefore, this type of physicalist ends up having to say that, yes, there are mental states, but, no, they have nothing to do with what occurs in the physical world. But that would mean that they do not really believe what they do about materialism due to the exis-tence of intention or reasons, but just because the physical world happens to be the way it is. If this is the case, then, there is no real reasoning.

Even if there are intentional or propositional states like beliefs, then these states have to be "epiphenomenal," without a causal role, or merely left unex-plained as the way things are, if naturalism is true. However, careful reflection on rational inference commits a person to the idea that one mental event or thought causes another mental event or thought by virtue of its propositional content.

If events are caused in accordance with physical law, they are so by being a particular type of event. A ball breaks a window because of its weight, density, and shape in relation to the physical structure of the window. Even if it is the baseball that Luis Gonzalez hit against Mariano Rivera that won the 2001 World Series, its being that ball has nothing to do with whether or not it can break the window now.

So let us suppose that brain state A consists of the thought that all men are mortal, and brain state B consists of the thought that Socrates is a man, and that together they result in the belief that Socrates is mortal. It is not sufficient for rational inference to exist that these states of mind consist of those beliefs, but it is required that the causal transaction, the deductive logic, consists of the con-tent of those thoughts. But, if naturalism is true, and if anything in physical space and time causes these thoughts, then the propositional content (all men are mortal / Socrates is a man) is irrelevant to the conclusion (Socrates is mortal), and we do not have a case of rational inference. In rational inference, as Lewis puts it, one thought causes another thought not by merely existing, but by the first being seen as the ground for the second.[13] But according to a naturalistic ac-count of causation, causal connections in the brain occur because of its being in a particular type of state that is relevant to physical causal transactions. Only a genuinely physical property of the brain can be relevant to what the brain does.

---

[13] C. S. Lewis, *Miracles*, 15.

Those forms of materialism that accept property dualism (unlike Cartesian dualism, the theory of the existence of a single, physical substance, which has two potential properties: physical and mental states) invariably render mental properties causally inert. If physical properties are sufficient to produce thoughts, then the mental properties are irrelevant unless they are really physical properties "writ large," so to speak. And mental states that are epiphenomenal cannot really participate in rational inference.

Carrier's account of mental causation clearly presupposes a reductive materialism:

> Every meaningful proposition is the content or output of a virtual model. . . . [A] brain computes degrees of confidence in any given proposition, by running its corresponding virtual model and comparing it and its output with observational data, or the output of other computations. Thus, when I say I "accept" Proposition A this means that my brain computes a high level of confidence that Virtual Model A corresponds to a system in the real world (or another system in our own or another's brain, as the case may be); while if I "reject" A, then I have a high level of confidence that A does not so correspond; but if I "suspend judgment," then I have a low level of confidence either way.[14]

Here again we find Carrier explaining one kind of mental activity in terms of another mental activity and then explaining it "naturalistically" by saying "the brain" does it. It is almost as if naturalists think they can use the magic word "brain" and naturalize any teleological function. That will not do. The use of brain-talk does not guarantee that the explanations are genuinely naturalistic.

The argument from the unity of consciousness is the notion that most mental experience entails a consciousness not of A and, separately, of B and, separately, of C, but of A-and-B-and-C together, the contents of a single conscious state. Consider what happens when I look out as I am driving down the road. I see the light turn red, I see traffic come to a stop in my lane. I conclude on that basis that I ought to slow my car to a stop. Common-sensically, there has to be one entity, namely myself, which sees the light turn red and traffic slow, concludes that I ought to slow down, and actually stops my car. But now consider what a person looks like from the point of view of materialism. According to that view he is not a single entity or unit but a functional conglomeration of physical particles, a

---

[14] Carrier, op. cit.

system of parts working together. What is it that makes a person a person? Is the total self we call "me" an illusion, something we can refer to for convenience but does not exist in reality?

Consider once again the inference "All men are mortal, Socrates is a man, therefore Socrates is mortal." Now if there is one person who has all these thoughts, then it might be supposed that a rational inference has occurred. But if Bill has the thought "All men are mortal," and Dennis has the thought "Socrates is a man," and I have the thought "Socrates is mortal," then no one person has actually made the inference, and so the inference never takes place. If there is no personhood, no unity of consciousness, then there cannot be any rational inference.

William Hasker, who has been the chief proponent of the argument from the unity of consciousness as well as the argument from reason, nevertheless thinks that these are separate arguments, and that the argument from the unity of consciousness should not be counted among the arguments from reason. Even Carrier agrees that the argument against naturalism from the unity of consciousness is really an argument from consciousness rather than an argument from reason, and that in the last analysis what is plausible in the argument from reason is simply the argument from consciousness. As Hasker has argued, "The issue of unity of consciousness, after all, applies to conscious states that are in no way concerned with reasoning, including the states of sentient beings incapable of reason."[15]

True enough. But some philosophers and scientists, confronted with the problem of the unity of consciousness, attempt to show that this unity is an illusion of some kind. According to Susan Blackmore, "Each illusory self is a construct of the memetic world in which it successfully competes. Each selfplex gives rise to ordinary human consciousness based on the false idea that there is something inside who is in charge."[16] This is clearly the claim that the unified self is an illusion and does not really exist. According to Steven Pinker:

> There's considerable evidence that the unified self is a fiction – that the mind is a congeries of parts acting asynchronously, and that it is only an illusion that there's a president in the Oval Office of the brain who oversees the activity of everything.[17]

---

[15] Hasker, "What About a Sensible Naturalism?" *Philosophia Christi*, ser. 2, 5.1 (2003), 54 n. 6.

[16] Susan Blackmore, *The Meme Machine* (Oxford, 1999), 236.

[17] Steven Pinker, "Is Science Killing the Soul?" *Edge*, 53 (April 8, 1999), 15. Available online at www.edge.org/documents/archive/edge53.html.

If this is really true, if there is really no one unified conscious that thinks the thoughts it thinks, then it follows straightforwardly that no one performs any rational inferences, including the rational inferences that have been used to reach the conclusion that the unified self is a fiction. Thus, the theory of a fictional self-hood is self-refuting. Thus, the argument from reason comes to the aid of the argument from the unity of consciousness by blocking a fictionalist account of that unity.

Can thought be "parted out?" Kant, in the *Second Paralogism*, argued that it could not:

> An effect which arises from the concurrence of many acting substances is indeed possible, for example, when this effect is external (as, for instance, the motion of a body is the combined motion of all it parts). But with thoughts, the internal "accidents" belonging to a thinking being, it is different. For suppose it is the "composite" that thinks: then every part of it would be part of the thought, and only all of them taken together would be the whole thought. But this cannot be consistently maintained. Certain representations (for instance, the single words of a verse) distributed among different beings never make up a whole thought (a verse), and it is therefore impossible that a thought should inhere in what is essentially composite. It is therefore possible only in a single substance, which, not being an aggregate of many, is absolutely simple.[18]

Kant did not think that this argument proves mind-body dualism, because he was prepared to make a distinction between the self as it is in itself and the self as it appears to us. But a modern materialist acknowledges only the self described by science; he believes that it is the real self. However, Kant's argument proved that a materialist/realist account of the self is impossible, although his own solution was not a dualist one.

Another form of Kant's argument, which is developed in William Hasker's essay "Unity of Soul, Unity of Consciousness" is as follows:

1. I am aware of my present visual field [physical surroundings] as a unity; in other words, the various components of the field are experienced by a single subject simultaneously.

---

[18] Immanuel Kant, *Critique of Pure Reason*, tr. N. Kemp Smith (New York: St. Martin's, 1865), 355 (A352).

2. Only something that functions as a whole rather than as a system of parts could experience a visual field as a unity.

3. Therefore, the subject functions as a whole rather than as a system of parts.

4. The brain and nervous system, and the entire body, is nothing more than a collection of physical parts organized in a certain way. (In other words, holism is false.)

5. Therefore, the brain and nervous system cannot function as a whole; it must function as a system of parts.

6. Therefore, the subject is not the brain and nervous system (or the body, etc.)

7. If the subject is not the brain and nervous system then it is (or contains as a proper part) a non-physical mind or "soul", that is, a mind that is not ontologically reducible to the sorts of entities studied in the physical sciences. Such a mind, even if it is extended in space, could function as a whole rather than as a system of parts and so could be aware of my present visual field as a unity.

8. Therefore the subject is a soul, or contains a soul as part of itself.[19]

Hasker's example is the synchronic unity of awareness of a visual field, but rational inference involves a diachronic unity: the inferring subject, who holds the premises of the argument in mind and draws the conclusion from them. It is not enough to point out that the brain is a highly complex system that is interconnected functionally and has billions of neurons. A genuine physical system is a system whose properties must be "summative" properties of its proper parts. If that is what a brain is, then no matter how complex it is, it is a unity of parts. A braking system of a car, a nutcracker, and even a chess-playing computer are all systems whose operations are the sums of the operations of their proper parts. But in human consciousness we find a subjective unity.[20]

---

[19] William Hasker, "Unity of Soul, Unity of Consciousness," forthcoming in *The Anti-Materialism Reader: Objections and Alternatives*, ed. George Bealer and Robert C. Koons (Oxford University Press). See also Hasker's *The Emergent Self* (Ithaca and London: Cornell University Press, 1999), 122–46.

[20] Hasker, *The Emergent Self.*

Carrier responds to this argument by claiming:

> But the point is the same: just as a collection of cells can organize and co-
> operate into a body that can walk – even though no one of those cells can
> walk at all or even has legs, much less the other needed organs, like hearts
> and lungs – so also can a collection of brain systems organize and cooperate
> into a mind that can think. And it does this by producing the virtual ap-
> pearance of a singularity of consciousness, just as it produces the mere ap-
> pearance that unified patches of color exist—when in fact only streams of
> various distinct particles exist.[21]

But the issue is not about a unity of function that can exist in a braking system, but a unity of perspective experienced by the thinking agent itself. When
a person infers "Socrates is mortal" from "All men are mortal" and "Socrates is
a man," that person infers the conclusion from his own perspective. There are
truths that we know from a first-person perspective that cannot be known from
any other perspective. For example, the truth that "I am Victor Reppert" is significant from my own perspective but cannot be discovered from a physical perspective. By taking an outside, third-person point of view, something is invariably lost, a point made by Lewis in his "Meditation on a Toolshed,"[22] and also by
present-day philosophers like Thomas Nagel and Frank Jackson.[23] Therefore, the
unity of consciousness, and the first-person perspective that accompanies that
unity of consciousness, is something that is profoundly difficult for a naturalist
to explain. Nevertheless, if there is such a thing as rational inference, then the
unity of consciousness must exist. And, if it does exist, and it is better explained
by theism than by naturalism, then once again we have a good reason to prefer
theism to naturalism.

Lewis maintained that naturalistic accounts of rational inference would explain reasoning away. I maintain that in three important areas – intentionality,

---

[21] Carrier, op. cit.

[22] C. S. Lewis, "Meditation on a Toolshed," in *God in the Dock* (Grand Rapids, 1970),
212–15. Lewis in that essay delineated the difference between "looking at" (from an outside
perspective) and "looking along" (from within) and argued that a general preference for the
view from without (or objective view) to the view from within (or subjective view) would
result in the undermining of reasoning.

[23] Thomas Nagel, "What it is like to be a bat," http://members.aol.com/NeoNoetics/
Nagel_Bat.html; Frank Jackson "Epiphenomenal Qualia, with excerpts from 'What Mary
Didn't Know,'" http://members.aol.com/NeoNoetics/Mary.html

mental causation, and the unity of consciousness – the danger of explaining reasoning away is a serious one that naturalists do not know how to overcome. In order to overcome these three arguments from reason, naturalists will have to come up with better responses than those they have so far provided.

All My Dogs Before Me

BRUCE R. JOHNSON

D ogs? Did C. S. Lewis own dogs?"
       That casual question, raised at one of the organizational meetings of
the Arizona C. S. Lewis Society,[1] led to a rather obscure search. Was Lewis a
pet owner? It is well known that he had created two imaginary worlds filled
with talking animals: Narnia and Boxen. Less well known was his opposition
to vivisection. An entire chapter of *The Problem of Pain* deals with pain as experienced by animals. A bear at the Whipsnade Zoo, nicknamed "Mr. Bultitude"
by Lewis and his brother, Warren, appears as a minor character in *That Hideous
Strength*. The other two books in the Ransom Trilogy contain vivid encounters
between man and translunary beasts (both sentient and otherwise). Lewis obviously thought well of animals. But did he have any pets of his own to nurture
and deepen that affection? Yes he did, as his autobiography, diary, and letters
clearly demonstrate.

The following is a list of eight dogs and other pets that were part of Lewis'
household during his life, from boyhood to his death in 1963. The gradual com-
piling of this trivia provided some occasional moments of comic relief as the Arizona C. S. Lewis Society began to take shape. During future gatherings, there
are sure to be additional trivia amassed on the pets and other pastimes of Lewis
and his extended household.

---

[1] There were eleven organizational meetings of the Arizona C. S. Lewis Society leading
up to the workshop for the film premier of *The Lion, the Witch, and the Wardrobe* held on October 22, 2005. The organizational meetings were all held at *Rula Bula*, an Irish pub in Tempe,
Arizona, where Lewis would have been very much at home. The founding members of the
Society included Steve Beard, Grayson Carter, Bruce R. Johnson, and Kirk Sexton.

Top left: Jack, Mrs. Moore and Warnie with "Pat" and "Papworth" at The Kilns, 1930.

Middle: David Gresham, Jack, and Douglas Gresham with "Susie" at The Kilns, about 1957.
Both used by permission of The Marion E. Wade Center, Wheaton College, Wheaton, IL.

Top right: Douglas Gresham with "Ricky" after 1963. *Taken by Walter Hooper and used by his permission.*

Bottom: Lewis, Maureen, and Mrs. Moore with "Baron Papworth" on holiday in Cornwall, August 1927. *Used by permission of The Marion E. Wade Center, Wheaton College, Wheaton, IL.*

1. Jacksie (*c*.1900). "He is Jacksie." It is no secret that C. S. Lewis disliked his given Christian name, Clive Staples. While on a childhood holiday, he approached his mother, pointed to himself and declared, "He is Jacksie."[2] The nickname, later shorted to "Jack," would remain with him for the rest of his life. Often overlooked is that Lewis took the name from a small, neighborhood dog that had recently been run over and killed.[3] Lewis was fond of the dog, and thus his change of name served two distinct functions: it memorialized his affection for the animal, and it disposed of an unappreciated given name.

2. Tim (*c*.1908–22). "[A] barrel, on four legs."[4] At Little Lea, their childhood home outside Belfast, Jack and Warnie had a least three pets: a canary called Peter, a mouse known as Tommy, and an Irish terrier, Tim.[5] A brief, but tender tribute to Tim appears in *Surprised by Joy*.[6] He never, it seems, quite grasped the concept of going for a walk, or at least (unlike most dogs) he remained indifferent to the experience. As Lewis dryly explained, "He never exactly obeyed you; he sometimes agreed with you."[7]

3. Pat (1923). "I had left him alone for [only] five minutes." A canine of a very different disposition is found in the diary of C. S. Lewis.[8] Pat is mentioned in the diary no less than thirty times, usually in the context of going for a walk with his master. The dog was first acquired as a puppy on September 28, 1923, while Lewis was living on Holyoake Road, Oxford, with Mrs. Moore and her daughter, Maureen.[9] Some months later, when Lewis had stepped out of the room, Pat managed to consume half of a volume of Plato, which Lewis had been translating.[10] That put an end to Greek translation for the day.

---

[2] W. H. Lewis, "Memoir of C.S. Lewis," in *Letters of C. S. Lewis* (New York, 1975), 2.

[3] Douglas Gresham, *Jack's Life: The Life Story of C. S. Lewis* (Nashville, 2005), 2.

[4] C. S. Lewis, *Surprised by Joy: The Shape of My Early Life* (New York, 1955), 162.

[5] Michael Coren, *The Man Who Created Narnia: The Story of C. S. Lewis* (Grand Rapids, 1994), 8.

[6] *Surprised by Joy*, 162–3.

[7] Ibid., 163.

[8] Walter Hooper, ed., *All My Road Before Me: The Diary of C. S. Lewis, 1922–1927* (San Diego, 1991).

[9] Ibid., 269.

[10] Ibid., 284.

Afternoon walks were always a source of great pleasure to Lewis, even more so when a canine companion shared his routine. Typically, he would return home for lunch, walk the dog (or dogs), and be driven back to college by Maureen about 4:30 p.m.[11] Several other pets are also mentioned in the Lewis diary: a turtle named Henry (owed by a housekeeper)[12] and several cats, including Tibbie[13] and Biddy Anne, who, Lewis writes (in 1924), had "recently adopted us."[14]

4. Mr. Papworth (*c.*1922–36). "[P]louging *through* every wave like a tramp."[15] A third dog, christened "Mr. Papworth," "Baron Papworth," or "Tykes," became a favorite of both Lewis and Mrs. Moore.[16] In September 1927, Papworth accompanied them and Maureen on holiday in Cornwall, where his frolicking in the waves amused everyone.[17] A perceptive eye can discern the dog as the large dark object on Maureen's lap in the photo of Lewis, Maureen and Mrs. Moore taken during that trip.[18] On September 28, 1931, Lewis and his brother undertook the now well-known motorcycle trip from Oxford to the Whipsnade Zoo, in Berkshire, during which Lewis' conversion to Christianity was finally completed. Even in the midst of this large drama, a dog played a small role. Mrs. Moore, Maureen, and an un-identified Irish friend lagged behind the Lewis brothers in a much slower car. Accompanying them that day was Mr. Papworth.[19]

5. Troddles (*c.*1936). "The heartless treatment meted out to poor old Troddles."[20] The diary of Warren Lewis mentioned another well-loved dog from a later time, though little is known of him. Apparently, Troddles was

---

[11] Colin Duriez, *Tolkien and C. S. Lewis: The Gift of Friendship* (Mahwah, N. J., 2003), 40.

[12] *All My Road Before Me*, 412.

[13] Ibid., 271.

[14] Ibid., 288.

[15] Walter Hooper, ed., *The Collected Letters of C. S. Lewis, Volume 1: Family Letters, 1905–1931*(San Francisco, 2004), 724.

[16] Ibid., 683.

[17] Ibid., 722–4.

[18] For example see Walter Hooper, *Through Joy and Beyond: A Pictorial Biography of C. S. Lewis* (New York, 1982), 64; Humphrey Carpenter, *The Inklings* (Boston, 1979), 16.

[19] William Griffin, *C. S. Lewis: Spirituality for Mere Christians* (New York, 1998), 41–2.

[20] W. H. Lewis, *Brothers and Friends: The Diaries of Major Warren Hamilton Lewis* (San Francisco, 1982), 232.

displaced by a dog both Warren and Jack came to despise: the highly spoiled Bruce. Ten years after Bruce's death, when a meeting of the Inklings focused on the question of whether dogs would share in the resurrection of the dead,[21] it can safely be assumed that the Lewis brothers may have longed for a reunion with Troddles or Mr. Papworth, but certainly not with Bruce.

6. Bruce (1935–50). "Met J[ack] in the Cloister," Warren confided to his diary, "who gave me the joyful news, 'Bruce is dead and buried.'"[22] During her declining years, Mrs. Moore became obsessed with pampering Bruce, insisting (among other things) that either Jack or Warren take him on numerous walks each day. Sometimes Bruce would bark throughout the night. Often, he would relieve himself in Mrs. Moore's centrally located (and often overheated) bedroom; the stench would permeate the entire house. [23]

7. Susie (*c.*1951). ". . . the dog, being an honest, humble person, always has a bad [conscience]."[24] Susie appears in several photographs dating from the time of Lewis' marriage to Joy Davidman.[25] Joy also brought with her a Persian cat named Snip,[26] whom Lewis referred to as my "step-cat."[27]

8. Ricky (1962). "Very anxious to be friendly."[28] Ricky, a boxer, was the last dog Lewis owned. He shared the Kilns with Lewis and his brother, with Snip, and with a ginger cat named Tom, who was described humorously by Lewis as "a great Don Juan and a mighty hunter before the Lord."[29]

---

[21] The meeting was held on Thursday, 28 March 1946. Ibid., 186. For more on Lewis and the eternal state of animals, see Gregory Bassham "Some Dogs Go to Heaven: Lewis on Animal Salvation" in *The Chronicles of Narnia and Philosophy: The Lion, the Witch, and the Worldview,* ed. Gregory Bassham, *et al.* (Peru, Ilinois: Carus, 2005), 273-86.

[22] Ibid., 232.

[23] Colin Duriez, *The C. S. Lewis Chronicles* (New York, 2005), 242.

[24] C. S. Lewis, *Letters to an American Lady* (Grand Rapids, 1967), 38.

[25] See the photograph section in Douglas Gresham, *Jack's Life: The Life Story of C. S. Lewis;* and in Douglas Gresham, *Lenten Lands: My Childhood with Joy Davidman and C. S. Lewis* (San Francisco, 2003).

[26] Gratitude must be expressed to Walter Hooper for assistance in distinguishing between this cat and Sambo, an earlier Siamese cat owned by Joy. *Jack's Life: The Life Story of C. S. Lewis,* 64.

[27] *Letters to an American Lady,* 105.

[28] Ibid.

[29] Ibid.

This list of dogs is helpful in illuminating the chapter on animal suffering in Lewis' apologetic work, *The Problem of Pain*.[30] First, Lewis had pondered the problem of animal pain since he was a child. While still only three years old, the suffering and death of the much-loved Jacksie led Lewis to adopt the dog's name for himself. Second, Lewis grounded his theological inquiries on animal pain on firsthand experience, with his own beloved pets. He began chapter nine of *The Problem of Pain* by admitting that all we say about what animals may feel is speculative.[31] This and other theological speculation on beasts, says Lewis, "must be based" on what we observe in tame animals.[32] What he had observed in Bruce and in a feline contemporary was that they both "live together in my house and seem to enjoy it."[33] From this Lewis could speculate whether one of humanity's unfinished tasks was to restore peace to the animal world—a theme explored creatively in *The Chronicles of Narnia*.

Of course Bruce brought little by way of peace to Lewis over the next decade. His remark to Arthur Greeves after Bruce had died speaks volumes: "We have (thank goodness) no dog now."[34] This leads to a third point: Lewis attempted to live out his theology in everyday life even when it proved difficult. Caring for Bruce, like caring for Mrs. Moore, grew more difficult as the years passed. For Lewis, however, these were among the various responsibilities given to him by God: they were a small part in the divine plan to restore a sense of order and peace to the world.

---

[30] C. S. Lewis, *The Problem of Pain* (New York, 1948).

[31] Ibid., 117.

[32] Ibid., 126–7.

[33] Ibid., 124.

[34] From a letter dated 15 June 1950, in Walter Hooper, ed., *The Letters of C. S. Lewis to Arthur Greeves* (New York, 1979), 228.

Review Essay

WILLIAM GENTRUP

Lewis Agonistes: How C. S. Lewis Can Train Us to Wrestle with the Modern and Postmodern World. By Louis Markos. Nashville: Broadman & Holman Publishers, 2003. ISBN 0-8054-2778-3. Pp. xv + 174. $19.99 [paper].

How would C. S. Lewis "wrestle" with the challenges of secularism and postmodernism had he lived into the later 20th century? This is the question one hoped would be answered by this book, and to a certain extent it was answered. The author, Professor Louis Markos (of Houston Baptist University), shows how Lewis might address a few *post*-modern issues such as the New Age movement (or neo-paganism), structuralism/poststructuralism, and the deconstruction of language (further developed in a final chapter on the deconstruction of heaven, hell, and sin), but he also reviews Lewis' answers to a number of modernist, even classical, challenges and challengers to belief: materialistic science or naturalism, the problem of evil (and pain), and the unhallowed trinity of Darwin, Freud, and Nietzsche. One of Lewis' legacies is as a champion against modern secularism. He provided responses to its truth-claims, and many Lewis readers will be familiar with his rebuttals. But these debates are still with us in the post-modern age, so it is good to have them included in this book.

While not using a scholarly format (the volume has no notes, bibliography, or index), the author (an English professor) is nonetheless comfortable with discussing a wide range of erudite subjects, such as the Eleutherian mysteries, Enlightenment ideologies, Tertullian, myth, pre-Socratic skepticism, existentialism, Islam, Kant, William Blake, and Jacques Derrida, to name a few. The intended audience, particularly in the chapter on New Age philosophy and the Arts, seems to be the church, but taken all together the book speaks to "we moderns," that is, everyone who has lived through the latter part of the 20th century.

After a preliminary chapter describing Lewis' education and conversion, known to those who have read *Surprised by Joy*, Markos treats Lewis' confrontation with scientific naturalism. Many readers will be familiar with these arguments. Lewis "wrestled" with Darwin's claim that life resulted simply from evolution by impersonal, mechanistic forces. He countered this with the fact that some things in life did not evolve at all, such as the universal experience of "joy," that fleeting sense of something so beautiful, so real, and so memorable that it creates a taste for the transcendental that can never be satisfied by something material. It does not "evolve" out of physical needs like hunger or sex. This so-called "argument from desire" suggests that it is illogical for the universe to give us a longing for anything that can not be satisfied (e.g., hunger would be illogical if food did not exist); hence, this transcendental yearning points to a reality beyond the material world where it can be fulfilled.

Lewis also demonstrated how human morality is something that could not have evolved from material forces. In the face of modern claims that morality is relative, Lewis asserts (in *The Abolition of Man* and the first part of *Mere Christianity*) that the ethical systems of past civilizations (e.g., Chinese, Babylonian, Hebrew, Norse) demonstrate amazing similarity. Hence, they transcend cultural conditions—which were all different—representing a universal standard that becomes even more evident, by contrast, when a Hitler, a Stalin, a Jim Jones, or an Osama bin Laden attempts to push forward a new ethical system (e.g., that terrorism is justice). Their outrageous acts reaffirm common morality. To naturalists who claim that morals derive from natural instincts (self-preservation, procreation, or protection of one's family) or from genes (the so-called "altruism" or "selfish" genes), Lewis replies that this argument falters under normal life choices. "What happens when two natural instincts come into conflict—when we must choose to save our own life or the lives of our family?" (66). The dilemma can only be solved by an appeal to a third principle (*tertium quid*) by which to weigh the competing instincts. But this third principle cannot be another instinct or it would not be able to judge between the other two; it would instead merely compete with them with an equal claim to priority. Something superior to the instincts must decide what is right, and this is why we look to the common code of ethics.

Finally (though not discussed by Markos), Lewis posits that human reason or consciousness could not have evolved from physical processes. To gain the understanding and knowledge of the universe that moderns have requires being outside the brute, impersonal processes of nature. A corollary of this argument demonstrates that naturalism is self-refuting. If all our thoughts are solely the products of a mechanical process then they could not have been arrived at by reason. Yet naturalists say that naturalism is rational, and they use reasoning to conclude that all that exists is the product of blind, mechanical forces. But if naturalism is true there is no ground for trusting reason, since reasoning would then be merely the result of random accidents. Based on the general experience and trustworthiness of reason, though, we can say that naturalism is false, or, if true, we cannot know it is so by logical deduction since this is not possible under naturalism. Hence, we must assume that our rational capacity has a non-mechanical, conscious, intelligent source. All three of these arguments, then, challenge the materialist worldview.

In the next chapter on the New Age movement, Markos has Lewis address that population of "moderns" who are in the opposite camp of the materialists: pantheistic individuals who wish to see God in everything, who represent a counter-swing from secularism back toward the sacred. In their reaction against Enlightenment logic, reason, and science, New Agers see a connection in all living things and believe in a universe that is sympathetic to their lives. How can the church reach these neo-pagans? According to Markos' application of Lewis' ideas, the church itself needs to embrace a more "medieval" and less impersonal, mechanistic view of the universe:

> If we are to win back the neo-pagans, we need to rediscover our awe at the majesty of God and his Creation, an awe that has little to do with the modern warfare over worship styles, and everything to do with that breathless sense of the numinous that we first encountered in the nursery when a timeless tale from mythology or folklore or legend ushered us into the world of faerie.

Why "medieval"? We moderns must recapture the fully alive universe that Dante describes or (one might add) that Lewis does in one of his best academic works, *The Discarded Image*. Does this mean that we must believe in hermeticism, alchemy, or astrology? No, but we must believe the universe is more than the cold, dark, hostile, and lifeless place about which Lewis wrote reams of poetry prior to his conversion. Just as he made a 180 degree turn, so too must the church. The first space voyage in *Out of the Silent Planet* (chapter 5) well illustrates this "medieval" concept of the cosmos, in my view:

> He [Ransom] had read of 'Space': at the back of his thinking for years had lurked the dismal fancy of black, cold vacuity, the utter deadness, which was supposed to separate the worlds . . . now the very name 'Space' seemed a blasphemous libel for this empyrean ocean of radiance in which they

swam. He could not call it 'dead'; he felt life pouring into him from it every moment. How indeed should it be otherwise, since out of this ocean the
worlds and all their life had come? He had thought it barren: he saw now
that it was the womb of worlds, whose blazing and innumerable offspring
looked down nightly even upon the earth with so many eyes . . . No: Space
was the wrong name. Older thinkers had been wiser when they named it
simply the heavens.

So, if the church is to respond to this New Age challenge seriously, where does
it begin? On the cosmological level, one might suggest the Anthropic Principle
would be a good place; on the terrestrial, not just an appreciation of the beau-
ties of flower, field, forest, or horizon, but also a sense of kinship with nature, an
(eco)consciousness of how the earth manifests the Creator (not to mention our
responsibilities in caring for it) and how it contains spiritual lessons (see Jesus'
parables). The modern church should not overreact to horoscopes, tree-hugging,
or myths. Lewis himself came to faith after a conversation with Tolkien in which
he was convinced that Jesus was the true fulfillment of the ancient myth of the
Dying and Risen God. A star led the pagan magi/astronomers/astrologers to the
Christ Child. We must therefore recognize the universe's *sympathies* for humanity and restore our sense of wonder for it. At the very least, the church might
imitate the mutual bond implied in St. Francis' "Brother Sun and Sister Moon."
If it does not, as Markos suggests, it will be in danger of an unjustified fear of
natural life and its sacred revelry. Ironically, it is far too easy for Christians to behave, like secular scientists, as if the physical is all there is and to accept a mechanistic cosmos that obeys certain laws, something to be experimented with and
dissected, but that has no mystery or numinous presence. In the end, the neo-
pagans may have more to teach the church and secular modernity in this regard
than the other way around.

(Parenthetically, it should be pointed out, in agreement with Markos, that
the pantheists do make one important error: there is no transcendent Personal
God in pantheism; instead, God is everywhere, in the trees, hills, rivers, etc. In
this respect it is easy to be a pantheist because there is no sense of moral responsibility or accountability to a personal Creator. The universe is so big and abstract
that it is not fazed by individual moral failing. But the God of the Bible demands
our obedience, a Father whose heart breaks at the prodigal failings of his people
and rejoices when they return to him. Analogously, one might say that some
excesses of positional theology approach pantheism: God's grace is so large and
abstract that sin is hardly noticeable in this framework. Sin seems forgiven auto-
matically and impersonally, making the Personhood of God almost irrelevant.)

The problem of evil and pain is not a particularly modern or postmodern issue. It goes back at least to the Book of Job. In chapter 4 Markos begins by citing the Enlightenment's inadequate response to the problem of evil and suffering. It posits that humanity is perfectible and that through the benefits of science, technology, and social planning a terrestrial utopia is possible. As we all have observed, from Marx to Skinner and all the totalitarian despots in between, this hope of total justice, equality, and relief from poverty and its deprivations appealed to millions. The crushing of individuality seemed an acceptable trade-off, but what also undermines such utopianism, Markos claims, is its basis in determinism. Darwin, Freud, Marx, Skinner and others all believed in some form of determinism—biological, psychological, historical, or political. If human nature is determined, and thereby freed from choice, it is freed from moral standards. As the 20th century alone can illustrate, numerous utopian dreams have turned into modernist nightmares, and no such dream has come close to achieving its promised results.

What is the Lewisian answer, then, to these modern efforts to discount pain and suffering? It is God's free will "experiment." Because choice allows for the possibility of sin, of rejecting God's will through asserting self-sufficiency, it also allows for suffering. Suffering and evil *exist* because of wrong choices; they cannot be wished away by deterministic utopianism and a belief in humanity's perfectibility. Lewis' emphasis on free will necessitates his rejection of the doctrine of predestination (and total depravity)—which he does. For Lewis, choice corresponds to the way things are: physical bodies, other choice-making individuals, and a "fixed" natural world. To ensure real and meaningful choices there must be interaction and resistance. Bodiless selves would not work as well as embodied ones to create encounters, and a controlled environment is also required for the experiment to work. If the natural world could change on a personal whim, then that person deprives others of their free will. Hence, nature must be unyielding (except when God performs a miracle) as a constant for the collision of choices to have meaning. But even the innocent suffer, so pain has another redemptive purpose. It is God's "megaphone," a way of getting us to listen to Him over the din of our "clamorous egos." It is also a road to wisdom, part of God's grand enterprise to form a "spiritual animal." Godliness after the Fall is meant to be accompanied by suffering, but whatever its form, we have the consolation that Christ always shares it.

In chapter 5, "Wrestling with the Arts," Markos returns to postmodern issues. One of the more fundamental postmodern attacks against the truth is the deconstruction of language itself. Ferdinand de Saussure and Jacques Derrida are the most prominent figures in this regard. (In the following discussion the use of the structuralist linguistic jargon of "sign," "signifier," and "signified" is purposely avoided.) To posit that words, the most basic unit of thought, are socially constructed and have no fixed meaning, that communication is therefore uncertain at best and unattainable at worst, is completely to undermine linguistic efforts at truth, not to mention the authority of sacred texts. In Saussure's system language is existentialist. There is no pre-existing Platonic essence or abstract reality for words like "beauty" and "truth," such as Beauty and Truth. Instead words are social products; the individual cannot invent or use language apart from the linguistic structure given to him. Beauty and Truth in one language will differ somewhat in meaning from the equivalent words in another language because the sounds differ as well as the contexts from which these sounds arose to be connected to concepts. For example, "bread" in English does not convey all the same connotations as "pain" in French. Thus, the power of words to transcend their socio-economic temporal structures and reach for transcendent and unchanging truths, such as in great literature or in Scripture, is viewed as "illusory" in this system. Language derives from the bottom up (i.e., human evolution) and not from the top down (i.e., divine gift).

Derrida took this analysis a step further. He posited that whenever a meaning is sought for a word, what is found is just another word pointing to another meaning which point to another word and another meaning, *ad infinitum*. Meaning is constantly deferred to other words with their meanings. There is no end to this quest. If we think of this as a search for the *center* of meaning, Derrida asserts that the center keeps shifting or that there is no center at all. Linguistically speaking, "there is no there there" (Gertrude Stein's familiar quote seems to fit nicely here). Hence, certain meaning is an illusion insofar as the search for it means the attempt to ground or freeze the meaning of a word. If we put the word "God" into the poststructuralist equation, we can see how Derrida and Saussure have problematized the search for meaning.

How would Lewis have addressed this postmodern challenge on behalf of Christianity? Markos first suggests that part of the problem of this attack on the transcendent power of language, power that might also be located in great poetry, has arisen because evangelicals "have not fought for poetry with anything like the vigor they have fought for creationism or biblical morality or the authority of Scripture" (119). This is especially ironic since the Bible is composed of poetry and literary narrative and employs numerous literary devices. But the Protestant (and, one might add, even earlier) distrust of metaphor and imaginative literature goes back to a distinction between a poetic view of inspiration and a "scientific" view of inerrancy. Markos is to be commended for being true to his profession (and Lewis') in raising such a point. A modern "Christian defense of poetry," as a phrase, is almost unimaginable in the evangelical church. Yet such a stance might have countered some of the poststructuralist skepticism rampant in academic and philosophical circles today.

When Markos returns to discussing how Lewis himself might have countered deconstructionism, he makes it clear that Lewis never directly addressed the issue. But he goes on to attempt an "aesthetics of incarnation" to challenge such views and cites some of Lewis' fiction to show how this incarnational aesthetic has been put into practice. First, Markos allows, imaginative literature plays the structuralist game by agreeing that language is fluid and not static:

> One the one side, then, we have conservative evangelicals who argue that language is meaningful because it is not slippery; on the other we have liberal theorists who claim that it is slippery and therefore meaningless. In the center, I would suggest, we have poetry that cries out on the rooftops that language is more meaningful precisely because it *is* slippery. Indeed, poetry, with its desire to incarnate transcendent truths in material images while yet maintaining via metaphors, symbols, allusions, and other devices a vital sense of play and interchange between the two, comes much closer than science or logic or even systematic theology to capturing and embodying the mystery inherent in the Incarnation. (130)

Incarnational aesthetics actually describes well a favorite New Testament and medieval form of biblical exegesis: typology. What is a typological interpretation like "Christ is our Passover" but a poetic identification of the literal with the figurative? In this sense, the Bible frequently allows a word or event to have multiple meanings, but it is never deconstructionist, ending in nihilism. Embodying universal truths in concrete forms, which the arts do, is *analogous* to the Incarnation. Markos strongly implies that it is the job of the church to celebrate and preserve the arts if only to provide a witness to poststructuralist skeptics of the possibility that the transcendent can be found in the material, that meaning can be located in words and art. Such assertions are already behind the church's current use of icons, liturgy, and the theology of the Incarnation itself.

Markos offers an illustration of this incarnational art from Lewis' novels. Just as, we recall, Lewis' own reading of George MacDonald's *Phantastes* baptized his young imagination, so Lewis' fiction can serve as examples of incarnational aesthetic to our imaginations. Lewis created worlds in Narnia that *parallel* salvation history; by doing so he engaged in an act of "redemptive deconstruction". He disassociated the usual terms of Christian theology (e.g., Christ, the Cross, the forbidden fruit) and attached them to new terms (e.g., Aslan, the Stone Table, Turkish Delight) with the narrative power to reinvigorate and inspire the traditional meanings of these terms. By doing so, he helped to reinvigorate the system of words and meanings. Instead of dead letters, these words now take on new and fresh meanings, reasserting the possibility of transcendental signification. Markos' argument here suggests the radical idea that there is nihilistic deconstruction and there is salvific deconstruction. The church need not fear the latter.

The book concludes with a discussion of "final" things: heaven and hell. The diminishing or deconstructing of the reality of heaven and hell is one of modernity's most devastating achievements. According to Markos, this has one of two sources. The first is the Enlightenment insistence on egalitarianism. Since everyone is equal, no one deserves to be treated differently than anyone else, and this includes one's ultimate destination as well. Another such doctrine based on equality is that no one can judge another person. Thirdly, Enlightenment determinism comes into play. Some behavior is ascribed not to choice but to biology: a selfish gene, a violent gene, or an infidelity gene. Hence, individuals may absolve themselves of bad choices by blaming them on societal or genetic forces. By exalting equality and undermining individual accountability for one's choices, the modern world deconstructs heaven and hell as places of ultimate reward or punishment, and their absolutism is simply regarded as unfair or untenable in the face of egalitarian relativism.

Another way of thinking that has brought heaven and hell into disrepute today is the view that both are merely states of mind. Reality is just a matter of perception. William Blake and Nietzsche saw hell as the bogey man of a "religious, Pharisaical world view that exalts reason, order, and obedience and demonizes energy, creativity, and excess" or as a "slave ethic used by the weak to keep the powerful in check" (149). In other words, heaven and hell are not real places but constructions imposed by others. One might add that the ubiquitous notion that hell is a place of fun, where one will "hang out" with one's likeminded friends and acquaintances, and that heaven is dull, is a derivation of this historical idea.

Yet another Enlightenment concept is the notion that utopian dreams have replaced heaven. Paradise should be on earth or not at all. When war, poverty, and ignorance cease, so shall immorality and everyone will be equal. Such a vision does away with hell and the need for a heaven, substituting humanity and earthly pleasure for God as the ultimate source of fulfillment. As might be expected, in order to believe that such a utopia can exist, the modern world must also deconstruct sin, an impediment to a view of perfectibility in this life. This dismissal of sin springs from the diminishment of free will.

Lewis' way of reinstating heaven and hell is to show them as, essentially, destinations settled by individual choice, thus dismissing egalitarian concerns, determinism, and utopian desires all at one go. Nor can they be viewed as punishment or reward disposed by another if they are the result of individual choice. Each human being *chooses*, by his or her actions, to go to heaven or hell (one such choice, given humanity's limits to do good on its own, is to participate in God's grace or reject it). Lewis illustrates this point in *The Problem of Pain*, *The Screwtape Letters*, and, most brilliantly, in *The Great Divorce*. In *The Problem of Pain* the great gamble God made in creating humans with free will means that he took a risk that some would reject him for the sake of a craving for independence or freedom: "the door of hell is locked on the inside," Lewis asserts, not on the outside (by God). Instead of annihilating us, Lewis construes that God, out of love, creates a place in the universe where he is absent, so that "all who do not desire to spend eternity with him may have a place to go" (152).

But how could someone ever get to the point where they would choose hell or separation from God? To answer this Lewis explains the psychology of sin. In *The Screwtape Letters*, Wormwood is taught that the best way to damn a soul is not through big sins, but through small ones. Their accumulation produces a gradual, imperceptible (to the sinner) decline into dehumanization. The various ways in which one can dehumanize oneself are dramatized in *The Great Divorce*. Here we see how our humanity is slowly whittled away by indulging and nurturing and letting grow some particular sin until it becomes a central part of our being, our identity, our reason for living. It could even be a good or harmless activity, but if it is put ahead of or in place of God, it detours into a form of fanaticism and becomes an idol. Whenever we choose ourselves over God we eventually lose our humanity. Each significant choice we make transforms us, bit by bit, into a heavenly or a hellish creature.

The "case studies" in *The Great Divorce* vividly reveal how humanity is dissolved by sin. The self-pitying woman who grumbles about every petty thing has become a Grumble. The artist who enjoyed capturing the numinous in landscape is now only the "Artiste" who loves the act of painting for its own sake. The mother who makes her love for her son her only meaning in life, transforms herself into the Mother of All Doting Mothers. It is not that such cases are expressive of any great evil. But that is the point. What is diminished is one's humanity; what was whole fades to a shadow of a self. If there is an ounce of anything left to be saved, an ember, a spark of humanity, one can be sure that the grace of God is ready to fan it back into a flame. In Lewis' vision of hell, the spirits are smudges, ghosts, without a shred of humanity left. Even if God could override free will, there would be nothing left to save in a damned soul. Lewis' hell is also

> almost completely devoid of people, for the residents of hell are so quarrelsome and self-centered that they cannot bear to live more than a few days in close proximity to a neighbor. . . . In hell there is neither community nor family nor friendship. There is only eternal narcissism. (163)

This is the psychology of sin taken to its logical extreme.

What has brought heaven into disrepute today? Two of modernity's main knocks against it are Freud's "wish fulfillment" and Marx's "opiate of the people" (spoken of religion in general, but pie-in-the-sky escapism is their real target). Both dismiss heaven in favor of earthly rewards and realities. But those who deny heaven for the sake of building a heaven on earth and seek an earthly immortality apart from accountability to God are engaging in the real wish fulfillment (166). The possibility of earthly utopias is proven false by history, and so the accusation of heaven being just a case of wish fulfillment or escapist fiction is mooted by the fact that the accusers are more guilty of the charge.

The proper response for Lewis and the modern Christian to the discrimination against heaven is to celebrate it, to envision its magnificent, life-affirming features and its human-fulfilling capacity. The modern church is sometimes embarrassed by talk of heaven because it has been so deconstructed by secularism, but this is a mistake. If heaven is our home, our end, goal, and consummation, and if we were not created to live forever in this fallen world, then believers need hardly feel guilty for rejoicing and proclaiming the glories of heaven. In fact, as Lewis is keen to remind us, earthly life cannot offer us any pleasures greater than those of heaven. If moderns cannot imagine them, it is because our desires are too weak, not too strong. Markos quotes from Lewis' celebrated Oxford sermon, "The Weight of Glory":

> We are half-hearted creatures, fooling around with drink and sex and ambition when infinite joy is offered us, like an ignorant child who wants to go on making mud pies in a slum because he cannot imagine what is meant by the offer of a holiday at the sea. We are far too easily pleased. (169)

Lewis' inspired portraits of heaven are, of course, the opposite of hell's. There humanity is fulfilled to the utmost. The afterlife is anything but claustrophobic.

The sheer size of heaven, with its constantly expanding vistas and deepening horizons as described in the last book of the *Narnia Chronicles*, matches the invitation to explore "farther up and further in." Not only the geography of heaven but also our new bodies and souls will undergo a profound expansion. Sounding very Lewisian, Markos adds,

> I fancy that when Christ said that in heaven we shall neither marry nor be given in marriage (Matthew 22:30), it was because heaven is a place where our capacity for love will be so enlarged that we will be able to love all our fellow heaven dwellers with greater ardor and *agape* love than we could the single spouse to whom we were wedded on earth. (169)

One's humanity can only grow in such an environment: "To enter heaven is to become more human than you ever succeeded in being on earth" (154). Heaven and hell are the ultimate fulfillment of personal choices, then. Both are ready-made alternatives of the love of God, allowing those who wish to see him face to face (by accepting his salvation) to do so and allowing those who wish to turn their backs to him to do so, also

In this volume Louis Markos has provided a service to C. S. Lewis scholarship. Although some aspects of the subjects addressed here have been covered elsewhere, few other authors have attempted to apply Lewis' thought so directly to the challenges of post-modernism.[1] This very well-written book succinctly covers the whole range of Lewis' important ideas and deserves to be read by all serious students of his work.

---

[1] But see Bruce Edwards, "Wise as Serpents, Harmless as Doves: Christians and Contemporary Critical Theory," *Christianity and Literature*, 39.3 (Spring 1990), 303-15 (with Branson Woodard); "Deconstruction and Rehabilitation: C. S. Lewis's Defense of Western Textuality," *The Journal of the Evangelical Theological Society* (June 1986), 205-14; and "C. S. Lewis and the Deconstructionists," *This World*, 10 (Winter 1985), 88-98. In "Lewis at 100," *A Visit to Vanity Fair: Moral Essays on the Present Age* (Baker, 2001), Alan Jacobs contends that the trend toward asking "what would Lewis say" about postmodern issues, such as postmodern critical theory, is "troublesome."

Upcoming Events

October 2, 2007
Arizona C.S. Lewis Society
Fall Book Discussion: *Mere Christianity*
7:30 p.m. on the first Tuesday of the
month at Quo Vadis Books
1037 E Lemon St
Tempe, AZ 85281
(480) 968-3663
www.azcslewissociety.org

October 6, 2007
Arizona C.S. Lewis Society
Fall Book Discussion: *Reflections on the
Psalms*
10:00 a.m. one Saturday per month
Tucson, AZ
520-908-0918
www.azcslewissociety.org

October 5-6, 2007
C.S. Lewis Foundation
National Faculty Forum
"The Crisis of the University: Religion
and the Future of the Academy"
University of Colorado, Boulder
www.cslewis.org

October 26-27, 2007
L. Russ Bush Center for Faith and
Culture
"C.S. Lewis: Man and His Work: A 21st
Century Legacy"
Southeastern College
Wake Forest, NC
www.sebts.edu/faithandculture

October 26-November 18, 2007
Northern Michigan C. S. Lewis Festival
Petoskey, Michigan
www.cslewisfestival.org

November 9-11, 2007
C.S. Lewis Foundation
Southwest Regional C.S. Lewis Retreat
"Seas, Islands, & Solid Ground: Navigat-
ing the False Infinites with C.S. Lewis"
Camp Allen Retreat and Conference Ctr.
Navasota, Texas
www.cslewis.org

May 29-June 1, 2008
Sixth Frances Ewbank Colloquium on
C.S. Lewis & Friends
Taylor University
Upland, Indiana
www.taylor.edu/academics/
supportservices/cslewis/colloquium

July 28-August 8, 2008
C.S. Lewis Foundation
C.S. Lewis Summer Institute –
Oxbridge 2008
"The Self and the Search for Meaning"
Oxford University and Cambridge
Universities, England
www.cslewis.org

October, 2008
Arizona C.S. Lewis Society
"C.S. Lewis: The Human Face of
Narnia"
Arizona State University
Northern Arizona University
Tempe and Flagstaff, Arizona
www.azcslewissociety.org

Submissions

Sehnsucht: The C. S. Lewis Journal welcomes submissions of articles, review essays and announcements related to C. S. Lewis and his writings from all interested parties in (but not limited to) the following disciplines: history, literary studies and criticism, philosophy, theology, apologetics, biography, medievalism, imagination, mythology, ethics, Christian spirituality, comparative religion, cultural studies, geography and philology (broadly defined). The journal is committed to the pursuit of the highest standards of academic research and writing, to the pursuit of truth, and to the advancement of the principles of "Mere Christianity" as articulated by Lewis. The journal is also committed to the encouragement of both traditional and more contemporary approaches to the study of Lewis, and, in that pursuit, to the consideration of diverse (and emerging) methodologies. All submissions will be evaluated in light of these considerations.

Submission should be made in writing to: The General Editor, *Sehnsucht: The C. S. Lewis Journal*, Fuller Theological Seminary SW, 4646 East Van Buren Street, Phoenix, Arizona 85008. Informal inquiries to the General Editor are encouraged, and can be made by e-mail at gcarter@fuller.edu.

Copyright

Style Sheet

Font size
- Articles/reviews should be printed in 12-point type, using Times New Roman.

Margins
- Top and bottom margins of *each* page (including the first page of text) *should not exceed 1 inch.*
- Side margins of each page *should not exceed 1 inch.*

Line Spacing
- Unless otherwise directed, all submissions should be double-spaced. Block quotations and footnotes should be single-spaced.

Punctuation
- Every sentence, including those in content footnotes, should end with a period, followed by *two spaces* before the beginning of the next sentence.

Hyphenation
- Care should be used in hyphenating compound words; to be certain of proper form, please consult a scholarly dictionary. *Do not hyphenate words at end of lines.*

Names
- The first mention of any person should provide the full (i.e., first and last) name. In subsequent references, use the surname (last name) only.

Paragraphs/Indention
- Indent each new paragraph five spaces (type on sixth space).
- Do not add extra (line) spaces between paragraphs.
- Do not indent the first line of block quotes.

Page Numbering
- Page numbers should be typed in Arabic script and placed at the top center of each page of written text.
- No page number is used on the first page of the text.

Page Numbers
- Please note the following examples of the use of page numbering in footnotes.
- 1-9.
- 11-19.
- 20-9.
- 111-19.
- 120-9.

Using Numbers in Text

- Spell out all numbers up through one hundred—e.g., sixty-five, ninety-eight—and all round numbers that can be expressed in two words—e.g., one hundred, two hundred, five thousand, forty-five hundred.
- Exact numbers over one hundred are written as figures—e.g., 102, 203, 304.

Quotations

- All quotations must be properly footnoted and placed in the text in an appropriate manner.
- Except in unusual circumstances, secondary works should not be quoted. Instead, paraphrase secondary source material and footnote it.
- Quotations are identified in two distinct ways:
  - Short quotations (45 words or less) should be included in the text, and designated as such by use of double quotation marks at the beginning and end of a quote. (Use single quotation marks within double.) Words or expressions within the quotations that are added/not attributable to the author should be placed within brackets (not parentheses).
  - Longer quotations (greater than 45 words) should be placed in block quotes. The entire block quote is to be indented from the main text, single spaced, and be written in 10 point font *without using quotation marks*. The first line of a block quote is *not* indented.

Foreign Words

- All foreign words used should be italicized (or underlined, if necessary).

Capitalization

- As a general rule, only the first word of a sentence and proper names/nouns should be capitalized. If in doubt, do not capitalize a word. For example, "Bible" is capitalized, but "biblical" is not; "church" is not capitalized, but "Church of England" is.

Footnotes

- Footnotes (as opposed to parenthetical citations following the quotation) should be used.
- First name followed by last name (of author or editor), followed by a comma, title, etc.
- Include the place and date of publication.
- Omit "p." when indicating page number(s).
- Title should be italicized (or underlined if necessary).
- Use "Ibid." when citing *precisely* the previous footnote.
- Use 10 point font and single space.
- Short title: After the initial citation of a work, use short title form on *all* subsequent citations.
  - Examples:
    1) **One author**: Napoleon Bonaparte, *Who Won Waterloo?* (Oxford, 1998), 27.
    2) **Two authors**: Charles Stuart and Oliver Cromwell, *The English Civil War* (Cambridge, 2001), 121-2.

3) **Editor**: Thomas Babington Macaulay, ed., *History is Bunk* (Cambridge, 2001), 678.

4) **More than one editor**: Sam Thick and Bill Bonkers, eds., *The Intellectuals* (New York, 2002), 89-405.

5) **Multi-volume work**: Chris Columbus, *America, My Home*, 10 vols. (Oxford, 1998-9), 5:467-9.

6) **Journal Articles**: Richard Nixon, "I am Not a Crook," *Vanity Fair*, 1994, 11.

7) **Internet sources**: www.seminaryworld.com

8) **CD-Rom**: Helmar Junghans, *Martin Luther*, CD-Rom (Minneapolis, 2002).

9) **Short title**: Always use short-title form for all subsequent citations. Thus, the first time the work is cited use: Ulrich Zwingli, *Luther the Heretic* (Phoenix, 1998), 22. After that, use: Zwingli, 23. Sometimes the need arises to cite more than one author with the same last name. In that case, in subsequent citation(s) include his/her first name/initial in order to distinguish between the two individuals being cited.

10) **Ibid**. Always use "Ibid" (not "ibid"), followed by a period and comma, when the citation is identical to the previous citation (even when the page number may differ). Thus: Ibid., 12; Ibid., 23.

Internet Sources
• Internet sources must be cited fully and clearly in footnotes (see above).

Submission
• MS are to be submitted to the editor in either hard (paper) or electronic form (e-mail attachment; MS-Word or PDF file). Addresses provided above on *Call to Contributors* page.

General Notes
• **Contractions.** Please avoid use of contractions.
• **First Person.** The famous English historian Edward Gibbon once described "I" as "the most disgusting of pronouns." Thus, please avoid use of first person whenever possible.
• **"Said/says."** In general, avoid the use of such expressions as "C. S. Lewis said...." As Lewis' speech was recorded on only a few occasions, it is rarely possible to know what he actually *said*. It is possible, however, to know what he *wrote*. Thus, write: "C. S. Lewis wrote...," or "C. S. Lewis argued...."
• **"Felt/feel."** Likewise, avoid the use of such expressions as "Lewis felt...." While it is quite legitimate and even helpful to attempt to get inside the head/mind of a historical figure, the temptation of engaging in what is often referred to as "psychohistory" — or, the attempt to explain past events in psychological terms, should be avoided. Thus, please avoid whenever possible use of terms such as "felt" or "feels." Use instead: "C. S. Lewis wrote...," or "C. S. Lewis is alleged to have argued...."

- **Passive voice**. Events, ideas and issues from the past are often very complex, as are our attempts to explain them. Although active voice has of late become more widely used, it is often the passive voice that is the most effective way to convey the complex and nuanced interpretation of events, ideas and issues connected with Lewis. For example:
  - *Active Voice*: "C. S. Lewis loved Joy."
  - *Passive Voice*: "Joy was loved by C. S. Lewis." Or, "C.S. Lewis was emotionally very attached to Joy, and may in time have come to love her."
- **Split infinitives** should be avoided.

Quo Vadis Books

1037 E. Lemon Street
Tempe, AZ 85281
(480) 968-3663
quovadisbooks@qwest.net

A nonprofit Christian book ministry by the Tempe campus of Arizona State University since 1973. We carry
- A large C.S. Lewis section
- Books in apologetics, philosophy, science and theology
- The Bible in over 80 languages

"More Than Just A Bookstore"

Quo Vadis is "more than just a great bookstore." It's a comfortable place for study and worship, ministry and prayer, friendship and conversation, music and art. Come experience it!

Call about our C.S. Lewis reading group.

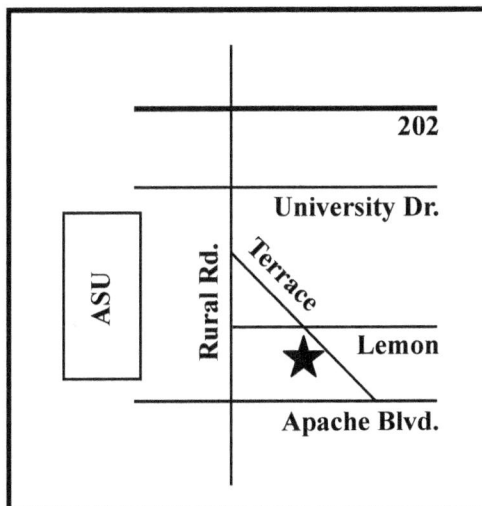

Subscription Form

Please photocopy the form below and send it with your payment to:

The Arizona C. S. Lewis Society
c/o Scottsdale Presbyterian Church
3421 N. Hayden Road
Scottsdale, AZ 85251

Make subscription checks payable to "Scottsdale Presbyterian Church."
Annual price: $20; students $10; institutions $30

NAME: _____

ADDRESS: _____

_____

_____

CREDIT CARD: _____ EXPIRATION: _____

E-MAIL: _____ SIGNATURE: _____

SEHNSUCHT: THE C. S. LEWIS JOURNAL

PLEASE INDICATE IF PAYMENT IS FOR

☐ VOLUME 1 (2007)

☐ VOLUME 2 (2008)

www.ingramcontent.com/pod-product-compliance
Lightning Source LLC
Chambersburg PA
CBHW071116090426
42737CB00013B/2603